UNHEARD VOICES

For my missing people, the talking hands and gentle voices inside my own story:
my mother Evelyn, father Arthur and
brother Lloyd Hately.

UNHEARD VOICES

Finding language and belonging in the Deaf and hearing worlds

Dawn Mauldon

CONTENTS

PART ONE

The users of a language, above all, will tend to a naïve realism, to see their language as a reflection of reality, not as a construct.

– Oliver Sacks, *Seeing Voices*

PROLOGUE

There are multiple voices and perspectives of beginnings, middles and half-finished endings. The gathering and rediscovering of family stories has influenced my own experiences and interpretations of people, places and language.

I was once called a 'connoisseur of people', but at the time the phrase was not meant as a compliment. Today, however, when I reflect upon the influence of my childhood experiences, I understand that people and stories have always been my passion, process and purpose. My curiosity about those around me has encouraged me to ask questions around language and culture, and how they can offer us a sense of belonging while at the same time exclude us from larger narratives.

For much of my life, my world consisted of two parents, two languages, two cultures and two places of belonging – an aural world and a visual world – existing side by side. There was much that I did not and could not know – what it was like to be born different, or to have a child who was born different. But I did learn what it was like to have parents who were considered different in the world in which we all lived together. There came a time when I needed answers for myself, if only to give others a reason for this difference in my life. But I never thought to ask other children like me how they interpreted their two worlds.

Some stories leave a mark on history, with particular experiences interpreted by others. In telling my mother's story, I have the opportunity to celebrate the forgotten – those who made sacrifices to find another language and culture for a child who could not fully participate in theirs. Believers who were challenged and compromised by circumstances deserve their rightful place in history. They also deserve to be forgiven, even if they found it hard to forgive themselves.

My mother, Evelyn, was born a child of difference who left her gentle imprint on each one of her landscapes of belonging. Voices that have been unheard are now gathered together to tell her story from one particular point of view – mine.

1. FATHER AND DAUGHTER

There are many stories waiting to be told, but the one for me has always been my mother's. Her family were farm people who never wanted water turned to wine, or loaves and fishes for a crowd. Instead, they made something from nothing every day. They were God's people who spread the word, led by example and shared what they had with due diligence and good grace. Inscribed in the old Lloyd family Bible were the words, 'In faith, not in hope.' Challenges descended upon this family of believers, faith and hope were tried and tested, and it was only belief that found a soft place to rest. The family was united in sharing the burden of their treasured cross, although the carrying of that cross was further for some than for others.

There was God, Nature, History and a little girl called Evelyn. Her father – my grandfather – was Arthur Leslie Lloyd. He loved words, he loved his family and most of the time he loved God, but it was actions more than words that belonged to this country farmer, especially when Evelyn came his way.

At that time, belief came and went with the weather, wars, births and deaths. Arthur understood the challenges of country life and had his own experience of war. In 1900, before he married, he had lived in South Africa where he became a member of the South African Light Horse regiment. Throughout that time, he wrote letters home. Those letters and his detailed diary captured another side to the man.

> *A few of the Victorians are camped near the town. I took a walk across to see if I could hear anything of Sam Cliver. Poor fellow, I was shocked when they told me he had been shot. He was a great favourite with the regiment and everybody spoke of him as 'poor old Sam'. He was the best fellow in the regiment. They all told me that he would share his last shilling with anybody and was always giving others a hand if they were a bit behind with their saddling up in the morning. I also saw Jack Lloyd of Greta, and others I knew.*

In 1917, the year my mother Evelyn was born, family and community were about praying, singing, lending a helping hand and working hard. She was the fifth and second-last child born to Arthur and Josephine 'Joey' Lloyd. Her siblings were, from oldest to youngest, Clifton, Gwenllian, Leighton and Adeline, with Evan coming along later. Together, they were one offshoot of the local Lloyd family, proud personalities living in Bobinawarrah, part of Victoria's Oxley Shire, and attending St Paul's Church of England (now St Paul's Anglican Church) at Milawa each Sunday. Their community of people were pioneers of routine, religion and responsibility.

For the Lloyd family, it was the unexplainable that required a closer understanding and some sort of acceptance.

Evelyn, at four years old, had not yet uttered one recognisable word.

Inside the family's busy farm kitchen, she observed her world. She seemed to be a perfect child, with a feathery frown, a halo of downy blonde hair and staring blue-grey eyes. Yet her tiny, silent presence provoked many questions.

Why doesn't she say any words?

Is she shy?

What is wrong with Evelyn?

Amid busy lives, some thought she simply needed more time and the family's patience to help her grow into her own voice. But Arthur and others guessed early what my grandmother Joey always struggled to accept: for Evelyn, the world was defined only by sight, touch, taste and smell.

A resolution to find a language for his daughter became Arthur's new sense of faith, hope and belief. My grandmother Joey often told me that in the early days Arthur carried Evelyn everywhere and never let her feet touch the ground. He had a sixth sense about her destiny; she was his priority and securing her future was his sole purpose.

The Lloyd family were Christian soldiers marching onwards. Opinions were best kept to yourself; family, God and community were how things must be done, on earth as it is in heaven. Arthur had his own opinion about Evelyn – nothing much wrong apart from her not sharing the language of others. He kept his thoughts to himself while he worked out what needed to be done. One thing he knew, though, was not to rush Joey. She seemed overwhelmed by Evelyn and her difference.

Farm life remained constant, but whenever Arthur could he would take Evelyn to the bend in the river. There they would spend time together, just the two of them, learning. Arthur made sure he was always clean-shaven, as instinct told him that a whisker-free face made it easier for Evelyn to see the shapes of words. He would hold her face in his hands, make sure she could see him, then say the words he believed.

'We're here by the river, Evelyn, to find you a voice. Everyone deserves that.'

In those days, platypus families still swam in the local rivers. The waterways whispered sounds of peace and harmony, but the mingled voices of the rivers and creeks also flowed over rocks, swept around logs, flooded muddy banks, crept into homes, destroyed roads and bridges, watered cattle, provided household water and, during drought, slowed to a trickle. It was also the gathering place for swimming, family picnics and storytelling. Joey once mentioned to me that Arthur's favourite hymn had always been 'Shall We Gather at the River'.

The river became the place where father and daughter discovered their language. Arthur could not explain his understanding of Evelyn. To him, her curiosity and intellect were not so different from those of his other children. Alongside her shy sense of fun and delight, she had her own way of making sense of farm and family life.

While Evelyn's gentle charm captivated Arthur, Joey tried to suppress her unease about her child. She felt as though Evelyn's difference was something personal against her. Joey wanted it to be someone else's fault, but in all the time that I knew my grandmother, there was never any doubt in my mind that she felt she was to blame.

Arthur would often announce, 'Joey, I'm taking Evelyn to the river. She loves watching everything around her there. It'll give you a break.'

The air in the kitchen would shift and shuffle. Arms folded around her waist, Joey would snap, 'I'd like time to wander by the river with a child to spoil.' She was always left out of the visits to the sanctuary where Arthur and Evelyn shared a language.

'Joey, I need to spend as much time with her as I can.'

'Don't be too long,' she'd say aloud, then mutter to herself, 'The river, for goodness sake. When there's so much to do here … He's always wandering away from what must be done.'

***

Evelyn's first language was touch. Gentle taps on her head, face, arms, shoulder or back would make her turn to a familiar hand, like another child would turn to the sound of a familiar voice. Although her family learned not to startle her, it was easy for people to become one big blur for Evelyn.

'One at a time,' Arthur would say. 'Evelyn gets confused if you all come at her at once.' Everyone tried too hard; that was the sort of people they were.

Peace for Evelyn was wandering by the river and reading one person only: her father. His tap was gentle, he would wait for her to look up at him before pointing and saying, 'Look, Evelyn.'

Her head would turn as quick as a roving robin. Arthur would observe her behaviours. She would look at birds perched on branches and then look down at their reflections in the sun-filled water. When he had her attention, he would take his index finger and thumb to make the movement of a bird's beak, experimenting. The soundless shape of his moving mouth was a visual match to the words, 'Bird, Evelyn.'

There were many more birds. Evelyn would giggle when her father showed her a bold, black-faced bird with wiry feet and a feathery coat of black-and-white threads embroidered with yellow and grey, and suspended upside down from a branch. A needle-sharp beak sipped nectar from spiky, apple-perfumed flowers. Arthur shaped the words, 'Evelyn, the acacias bloom after spring rains.'

My grandfather never questioned his unexplainable faith in Evelyn. It was much later that she would learn to spell bird and flower names, such as H-O-N-E-Y-E-A-T-E-R and A-C-A-C-I-A, with her hands. Yet well before then, he believed she would find the words for her own voice.

'Nothing much wrong with Evelyn that language can't fix,' Arthur would say over and over.

'How do we know which language she'll find?' asked Joey. She sensed that her daughter's words were somewhere in a faraway place.

'Optimism is what we need.' Arthur convinced himself, but perhaps not others.

Evelyn found many ways to interpret her world. A week

prior, her eldest sister Gwen had held up a hand mirror; the reflection of the two sisters had bounced back just like the birds in the water.

Moments on her own were rare for Evelyn. Even when she thought she was by herself, someone was always checking where she was and what she was doing.

'Watch her, Joey.'

Her parents stood together at the kitchen window, observing. Evelyn had taken that same mirror outside into the garden. She twisted and turned the circle of reflective glass to look at herself, the trees, the sky and the dog.

'Whatever is that child doing?' Joey asked, always on the lookout for signs of strange behaviour in her youngest daughter.

'Look, Joey, she's worked out that there are reflections to be found in the mirror.'

'Arthur, you're always trying to see the best in the child.'

'But it's clever to understand how the mirror works; she's finding ways to test its purpose.'

'And this is testing for me.'

'Joey, she's not a test, she's our daughter.'

'No-one knows that better than me. That's what you all forget.'

One afternoon at the river, when the time had come to leave and Arthur was gathering the horse, for once Evelyn's eyes did not follow him. He stopped and watched her. She was spellbound by the ripples on the river's surface. Arthur walked over to her side. Something quick had caught her eye and, not turning away, she tapped Arthur's leg.

'What is it, Evelyn? Mother will worry if we don't get home soon.'

Evelyn's index finger pointed to the flat shape of tobacco-brown velvet as it gracefully slipped through the watery shadows. There was a calm contrast she could see: the silvery swiftness of the darting fish between the waving reeds to that of a mammal with four feet used like fins to glide through the water. It was not a fish and not a bird, but a miracle in any language.

'A platypus! Oh, Evelyn, you saw it first! A platypus. Clever girl.'

Pride and pleasure were clear to her from the way her father's face moved and his gentle touch upon her head.

'My clever girl.' He knew that was not a word Joey used for Evelyn, but he thought she was a clever child in her own way.

Clouds crept across the Ovens River, sunlight withdrew into quiet spaces and the platypus vanished beneath the sound of Arthur's soft voice. 'Ready, Evelyn? Everyone will be looking for us.' Astride the horse, Arthur held the reins in one hand, and tucked Evelyn into his chest with the other as they headed for home.

2. FARM LIFE

On the horse ride back home to farm and family, father and daughter passed through the area where trees had been pushed out to make way for oats, hops, tobacco, wheat, sheep and cattle – the reshaped dreams of gold seekers and tin miners, the men and their families who had sailed from old worlds to settle land in this new-old world.

Those dreams were buried under yellow grass scorched by savage heat, cattle that needed protection from the flooding rivers and summer droughts, and farm life that depended on charitable weather and stubborn hope. There were never enough dreams to go around; compensation was land, community and working from dawn to dusk. Futures were restructured, the history of the land was retold, and people buried loved ones as they struggled to believe in the many points of difference in God's plan.

Farm language was the dairy cows gazing with brown-eyed longing over fences of rough wooden posts and stretched steel wire; the orchard of well-tended trees producing pears, figs, plums, lemons, oranges, mandarins and apples; and the grapevines providing shade for the walk to the outside washhouse and lavatory. Evelyn's playground included the entwined perfumes of creamy honeysuckle, pink roses, lilac petals, bold snapdragons, wild winter jonquils, apple blossom and delicate violets.

The four seasons dictated the fruits of the farm's labour, and Evelyn witnessed how the planting, pruning, picking, pickling, bottling, jam making, egg collecting, baking, milking, butter churning, and killing of animals for food was always punctuated with church, trips to town, picnics, family visits and celebrations like Christmas and Easter.

Food flavours and smells defined her days. Sunday was roast lamb with apple pie, Monday was shepherd's pie made from leftovers followed by vanilla custard and crisp bottled pears. Evelyn linked the dry smell of wheat country to her breakfast porridge, and to whenever her big sisters gave her wheat seeds to scatter for the chickens, ducks, turkeys and geese.

Evelyn's world was her family, food and the farm, as familiar to her as her own breathing. And she liked to be involved in small chores, like carrying the freshly picked vegetables inside and putting them on the table.

Seven-year-old Adeline said, 'See, Gwennie, she can do things.'

'Of course she can. But we still have to watch her.'

'Why? She won't go away.'

'Oh, Adeline. Wait until you're older, then you'll understand.' Gwen spoke with all the wisdom of an eleven-year-old and as an eldest sister.

'I can't wait!' Adeline would often get fed up with the constant chores. She was an innovative child who wanted to play and create things instead.

The old rooster, one bird Evelyn would never go near,

roused the rest of the household every day, but for Evelyn it was the sense of her family moving around the kitchen that woke her. In the first part of morning light, her brother Leighton would take her hand and shape the words, 'Evie, let's go outside.'

Eyes, nose, mouth and hands each had their own purpose, and so did ears in some way. Out in the yard, he'd place his hands over his ears and screw up his face, and she would laugh at what would come next. As he shook his finger at the bossy brown rooster, she'd watch the shape of his mouth.

'Evie, you hate that old rooster. So do I!'

Sometimes her attention travelled to the sheepdog resting at the back gate.

'Good dog, waiting to round up sheep. Patient and clever – just like you, Evie.'

'Time for breakfast,' someone would call. Leighton would point inside his mouth and Evelyn would follow him indoors to join the rest of their family. The day always started and finished around the sturdy kitchen table.

As the day stretched on, the chatter was about chores and meals, and as lunchtime neared someone would ask, 'Where's Evelyn?'

'I'll get her … Leighton, where is she?' Gwen always knew who to ask or where to look.

'She'll be outside watching the animals,' said Adeline.

'I don't know how she does it, but she knows not to wander away. She won't be far,' Leighton said.

'Oh, it's nearly lunchtime. She'll be at the gate waiting for Father,' Gwen realised.

Each day around noon, Evelyn waited at the back gate.

She'd first see the dog running towards the house, and then came Arthur. Light of step when he climbed down from the horse, she'd watch and wait while he led the animal to drink and graze. Then he would kneel down so she could see him say, 'Little one, up you come.'

'Here she is.' And through the back door they would come, with Arthur, smelling of cows and sheep, carrying Evelyn in his arms. Along with the smell of warm wool and damp cotton lining the wooden rail in front of the red brick fireplace, these scents would always remind Evelyn of her people, place and belonging.

Suspended safe in her father's arms, Evelyn was distracted by Leighton, who waved his hands to catch her attention and sang, 'Evie, you're king of the castle.'

'I think that's the *queen* of the castle, Leighton,' Arthur said, playing along. Evelyn's face would squeeze into the shape of joy, entrancing her father, sisters and brothers. But Joey was too preoccupied to be entertained.

Happy to be the centre of attention, Evelyn would smile and wave at her siblings. However, Leighton was quick enough to notice how Evelyn's face changed when Joey walked away.

'You can't put anything past Evie,' he'd say to Adeline.

'I'd like to see someone try.'

***

When Gwen and Cliff returned from early morning milking, Joey asked Gwen to dress Evelyn. Leighton had noticed that Evelyn preferred her sister dressing her, rather than their mother.

'In a minute,' Gwen replied.

'Now, Gwen,' Joey snapped.

'Joey, let Gwen have her breakfast first. Evelyn's alright for now,' interjected Arthur.

Although he understood that responsibility needed to be shared, it was hard to explain that to Gwen. A united parental front was imperative to keep them and the farm going.

'Mother, Gwennie has been up earlier than any of us this morning.'

'So have I, Leighton.'

'Gwennie, you take such good care of Evie,' Leighton said, acknowledging his sister's contribution.

'I wish we knew what to do about her,' whispered Gwen.

Leighton replied, 'Evie's smart, she watches everything. And she only has to see you to understand you.'

"That won't always be enough, Leighton.'

'It is for now.'

And that's where it rested. No-one, not even Leighton, was brave enough to be the one to name Evelyn's difference – at least, not within earshot of Joey.

3. LEIGHTON

Grandmother Wellington – Joey's mother and my great-grandmother – often visited the farmhouse, where the bustle of her opinions overloaded the congested kitchen.

'Don't worry about Evelyn, she's just shy,' Matilda Wellington said with sweeping authority.

Her mother had said this more than once in the last year, and Joey hoped she was right. It would make it easier if time and patience were the only things required to help Evelyn. But Leighton sensed that shyness was not the reason for his little sister ignoring the voices of her family.

'Mother, she's not shy with us. I think it's something else.'

'Not now, son.'

'Outside, Leighton,' Grandmother ordered. And he obeyed.

Fresh air helped him to think new thoughts about how language worked, beyond the spoken word. Over time, he started to realise how language could be visual, tactile, olfactory and theatrical. Evelyn was alert and easily entertained; it couldn't be too difficult for the willing to find other ways to communicate with her.

After their grandmother's visit, Leighton turned to his sister.

'You only want to be included, don't you, Evie?'

He pointed to the contented cat and devoted dog and mouthed, 'Sneaky cat. Loyal dog, Evie.' Evelyn smiled as if she'd heard every word.

Without sound, word shapes meant little to Evelyn. Everyone had tried them with her over and over again – 'C-A-T', 'D-O-G', 'C-A-T', 'D-O-G'. But no-one seemed to have words for what Evelyn already knew: the ginger animal spread across the fire's hearth was sly and self-centred; the bigger, fluffy one, often crouched at the back gate, was loyal and hardworking.

Evelyn was not ignored or forgotten, but others noticed her difference. Whispered words packed a punch. 'Retarded' and 'disabled' – words that implied either an intellectual or a physical impairment, words that easily merged into the one word – were interpretations of Evelyn that the Lloyd family did not want to hear or accept.

'What's wrong with Evelyn?' Cliff asked.

'Nothing's wrong with her,' Joey snapped at him.

Everyone would comment on how placid Evelyn was. That is, until she found a way to make herself heard. One day, Joey placed her on the small wooden chair with flowery cushions, saying, 'Stay there, Evelyn.'

Without any warning, Evelyn kicked the chair with her heels and slapped its arms. Her runny nose and soft crying gasps commanded attention.

'Mother, she doesn't want to sit still. She wants to play outside.' Adeline always spoke up for her sister. 'How would you like being made to sit still and watch everything that's going on?'

'Adeline, don't be cheeky. She used to be happy watching us.'

'Mother, she's getting bigger. She likes being busy.'

Joey wasn't in the mood for strong-willed daughters. Then light and Leighton came through the back door. When he waved to Evelyn, she stopped crying at once.

'Evie! Now what's going on here, little one?'

'Leighton, can you take Evelyn outside to play?' asked Joey.

'Come on, Evie. I'll take you to the orchard. Your favourite place.' It was in the orchard where Leighton had noticed that Evelyn seemed to understand things through taste, touch, smell and sight.

'Thanks, Leighton. I never know why she's upset.'

Adeline crossed her arms and planted her bare feet firmly on the floor. 'But Mother, I knew what was wrong with Evelyn!'

'Don't worry, I'm taking her outside now,' Leighton said, saving the day and Adeline's bottom.

'She'd follow that boy to the ends of the earth,' was Joey's response to the room.

Reprieved and relieved, Joey braced her shoulders, jutted her chin and prepared herself for the rest of the day.

Squashed in between busy lives, it was so easy for everyone to forget that Leighton was just a boy, with torn loyalties about his mother's pain, his father's wisdom, and the way his two sisters took on the mothering of their youngest sibling.

***

Kitchen life never stopped for weather or emotions. While Leighton looked after Evelyn, Gwen and Joey continued with their chores.

'He's the only one who can handle her whenever she's upset.'

'Of course, Mother. He has the time to be patient with her,' replied Gwen.

'Someone has to calm her down.'

'She's trying to tell us something when she gets upset.'

'Oh, Gwen, I know that, but I can never tell what she wants. Can you?'

'It takes time to work out. But we must try rather than pander to her.'

'Thank goodness for Leighton is all I can say.'

'Mother, it saves us time distracting her, but it's not helping us to understand what she's thinking or wanting. How must it feel when she can't explain herself?'

'That's enough, Gwen. I think of nothing else but Evelyn.'

'Mother, we all do.'

'Well, it wears me out. Come on, now. Those jolly cows won't milk themselves.'

The sun was out, and the path to the cowshed was dry. Gwen began to sing.

'*All things bright and beautiful … All creatures great and small …*'

Joey pulled her tatty, red felt beret down tight, her ears and fears covered. She joined her daughter and the two of them sang in harmony.

'*All things wise and wonderful … The Lord God made them all.*'

From the orchard, Leighton turned to hear the sounds of their soft singing.

'Listen, Evie,' he said. But she didn't hear what he heard.

***

Leighton had never-ending patience, like his father. They both listened to every rhythm, pattern, sound and silence that came from Evelyn's world. Both would first tap her on the head or shoulder, then wait until she made eye contact before giving her a small instruction or task to do. 'Come on, Evie,' Leighton had said, when he'd handed her a small fruit bucket to carry, and pointed: 'Orchard.'

In the orchard, brother and sister would sit hidden beneath the heavily laden branches of bold red apples, cocooned inside their own cubbyhouse – a country classroom from where they observed farm life taking place.

Evelyn watched as Leighton picked the perfect specimen, polished it on his woollen jumper and held it up like a trophy won in a picnic race.

'Here you go, Evie … Apple.'

Her shy smile said it all. She took the apple in both hands, held it to her nose to breathe in the crisp, sugary perfume, opened her mouth wide and took a big bite.

'You know what's going on, don't you, Evie?'

Leighton tried new things with words. He held his mouth big and wide for 'A', puffed his lips for 'P', made a soft smile for 'E'. Evelyn could see his tongue between his teeth for 'L' as he repeated, 'App … ell, app … ell, app … ell.' The soundless word of her favourite fruit.

In response, Evelyn stood on her tiptoes, reached up

for the best apple within her grasp, and then, mirroring Leighton's actions, stroked its smooth surface and rubbed it over her apron. Pleased with herself, she held her gift out to her brother, offering him the shiny fruit. Giving was the family way.

She pointed to her nose for him to smell the apple.

'Thank you, kind Evie.'

***

Sunday services, a large part of their life on the farm, offered Leighton some high hopes about God's plans for their family.

'For God so loved the world, that he gave his only Son, that whoever believes in him should not perish but have eternal life.' (John 3:16)

Each Sunday, Leighton saw heads turning towards Evelyn, staring, whispering and guessing. At home after the service, he would question this behaviour.

'Mother, why do people stare at Evie?'

'Leighton, I don't know. Sometimes I don't have any answers, not even for myself.'

'I thought we were all God's children.'

'Yes, Son. It doesn't stop people wondering about Evelyn, though.'

'She can't believe in God without having any words for that.'

'Oh Leighton, that's too much to try and understand.'

'It's not fair. Evelyn is a perfect child just as she is.'

He went outside and Joey was left with five minutes alone.

She slipped away into the quiet shadows of the dining

room to gather her thoughts. She surrendered herself down into the cracked leather armchair, the one with the buttons that Evelyn liked to touch. It was where she had breastfed all her children. A simple pleasure she remembered fondly. Once settled, she closed her eyes, hummed her favourite hymn and hoped to relax. But the sensation that brewed beneath her eyelids was not one of calm. It stemmed from something else altogether: sorrow.

***

People missing out bothered Leighton, and it felt like there was always someone missing out in the family, whether it was time, space, comfort or praise. Although it had not been discussed, everyone knew that Evie was missing out on hearing the sounds around her. But naming it would make it a problem that needed to be solved, and no-one was ready for that just yet.

In Leighton's mind, the spaces left by not hearing sounds could never be filled. Evie was missing out on the glorious sound of their mother's contralto voice rising above all others in church. Sunday choir was Mother's place to gather faith, hope, and share her God-given gift with everyone – except for Evelyn.

There were so many distinctive sounds apart from his mother's singing. Leighton loved the changing sounds of the weather. Wind whistling through the old willow by the creek, and how the warbling magpies warned of coming rain. Evie did jump or turn to the vibrations of angry storms that crashed and banged across the farm. Leighton was sure that of everyone he knew, it would be Evie who would also love the *pitter-patter* sound of a soft, soothing rain.

Although Evie never heard the *peep-peep* of the day-old chicks that Leighton gave her to hold, she could feel the warm heartbeat of the smallest handful of soft, yellow, downy fluff and it made her smile. He delighted in watching his sister hold the buttercup bundles that would grow into a busy hen or a bossy rooster. But Evie would miss the hen's cackle announcing another freshly laid egg.

Certain household sounds, like the footsteps on the floorboards that announced the end of a farm day and the last bang of the back door, meant everyone was home together. Domestic music was the friendly crackle of the fire heard between family chatter. Even the heavy black kettle made the simple sounds of home comfort as water sloshed inside it or boiling water splashed over tea leaves. Outside, the devoted dog snored to himself, tired from barking his master home. Inside, the contented cat purred to the murmur of family belonging.

And no matter how hard he tried, Leighton could never make up to Evie for all the missing sounds in her Bobinawarrah world.

* * *

Beauty, however, was another language for Evelyn, and Leighton knew how to share that with her through his gift for mime. Before they left home with Joey for their weekly visit to their grandparents, Leighton would stoop and shuffle in impersonation of the old people and, in a posh English accent, say, 'Evie we're going to Tea Garden Creek.' He would also hold up his hands to mime holding and turning a steering wheel. Through his precise performance, Evelyn easily understood that they were going to visit their grandparents, the ones who had a car.

On arrival at their grandparents' place, he would hold her up to touch the embossed brass word 'Waterloo' located on the left side of the front door. The shiny, bumpy-smooth shapes spelled out the noble name of the Wellington home.

Their grandmother's house always had large vases of flora in the passageway and the sitting room. The fresh blooms were picked from her colourful garden that overflowed with plants, birds and insects. Evelyn's favourite creatures in the garden were the dainty ladybirds that flew onto the roses to eat the aphids. Leighton would sing, '*Ladybird, ladybird, fly away home*', then place a pin-spotted droplet of red and black into Evelyn's open palm. Her tiny hand would stay open as the soft wings lifted into airborne magic.

'Ladybirds are lucky, Evie. People don't think you are lucky, but I do. Look, look! There's more …' Evelyn's eyes would follow the flying red-and-black buttons. Her chirpy chuckle was the softest sound that Leighton wished to hear over and over.

He wanted to believe that one day his sister would find her own voice and that of her own choir. Where that could happen, he was unsure. He discovered stories and performed them impromptu for her. He was a Lloyd boy, but for her he was a brother, director, entertainer, audience and guardian angel. That was enough for each day they spent together. Gentle Leighton always found a freedom of expression with Evelyn. And that was why he loved her so much.

4. THE LLOYD BOYS

To be born a Lloyd boy carried expectation, and the eldest son had more expected of them. Cliff Lloyd was that son. He had rosy cheeks and a cheeky smile and he loved his little sister like they all did. There were a few missing pieces in Cliff's good nature, such as Leighton's patience, Gwen's mothering and Adeline's practicality. Cliff was just a boy trying to navigate adult attitudes, and he preferred to take any opportunity to have fun or to escape family responsibility.

'What does she want, Leighton?' Cliff would ask, trying to understand his tiniest sister.

'Look at her, Cliffy, and work it out for yourself.'

'I can't, I don't know how. Tell me what she wants.'

'Think about it. You'll work it out.'

Leighton knew a lot, but there was something he never found out about a memorable afternoon in the cowshed when Cliff and Gwen had milking to do and Evelyn had joined them.

Cliff waved to get Evelyn's attention. Then he squeezed the cow's soft, pink teat into a pencil shape to draw a rainbow of shiny, creamy-white milk across the sky of the shed. The playful boy knew how to aim just far enough to land silky droplets right at Evelyn's feet. Gwen was busy cleaning the separator. She would never allow milk to be wasted, so it was only Cliff who heard the sound of his little sister's throaty giggle. He couldn't help whispering, 'Hey, Leighton, stick that in your pipe and smoke it.'

Cliff had worked out humour was his best way to connect with Evelyn.

***

The Lloyd family was integral to Bobinawarrah history through the story of the 'Farmers Five' – George Harry Brown, Robert Montgomery, Alexander Moyer Simpson, and brothers Frederick Bianchi Lloyd and Charles Westall Lloyd – who had all met at the Bendigo goldfields in their early twenties and soon became firm friends.

In 1857, they had the idea to buy land to farm in the Oxley Shire. They walked all the way from Chiltern to Wangaratta, arriving on Christmas Eve. The next day they crossed the Ovens River and settled the area now called Hurdle Creek. And that is when they became known as the 'Farmers Five'.

Vaughan was the firstborn son of Arthur's eldest brother, Charles Lloyd. As the eldest Lloyd boy in the whole family, he would inherit titles, stipends and status. Welsh and royal history rested on his fragile shoulders, the past and the future. A grandson of pioneering history, Vaughan was born without the wherewithal to make significant contributions, navigate or extend his bestowed family role, but he was born with enough naïvety to blurt out his own clumsy truths.

'Evelyn's taking a long time to say things,' said Vaughan to Leighton. 'There's something wrong with her.'

'No, there isn't. I know Evie better than anyone.'

Vaughan walked to Evelyn and shouted into her face, 'EVELYN, THERE IS THE DOG.'

'Vaughan! Don't speak to her that way! She doesn't like it.'

'How do you know?'

Leighton never intended to defend Evie against ignorance. Vaughan was not an unkind boy, only careless and uninformed. Lloyd children learned early about how to keep things to themselves. All except for Vaughan, who voiced what others did not dare. 'Do you think she can hear what we say?'

'She knows when you're talking about her,' retorted Leighton.

'How?'

'Some people don't hear, even when they have perfect hearing.'

'Leighton, I've got no idea what you mean.'

'No, you wouldn't. Evie understands more about people than you ever will.'

The dog had more sense and sensitivity than Vaughan and his own importance; at least, that's how both Leighton and Evelyn saw their cousin.

The expectations placed upon the older boys did not apply to Leighton. His place in history was the way Evelyn looked up to him. Joey's third child, Leighton Wellington Lloyd, carried his mother's grand expectations in his name, at once Cornish and Welsh, both families acknowledged.

Farming was the future for Lloyd boys, and it appeared to be Leighton's only option. Unsure why, Joey couldn't imagine him as a farmer or a minister. She admired teachers, and she could picture Leighton as a teacher. Perhaps it was to do with the way he was with Evelyn.

Although all the Lloyd boys had a soft spot for Evelyn and would do anything for her, Leighton's unique way of communicating with her made them feel awkward about their own approaches.

Mime has always been a visual and physical way of communicating language and culture; Leighton inherently understood that mime was a process for helping Evelyn to read her world. But she could always see the funny side of things when he performed for her. It was how he came to understand that humour and beauty were her guiding lights.

5. SISTERHOOD

While there was a place for everyone in the family, some areas were strictly off limits. Inside the church on any Saturday evening, when the women of the family gathered for rostered church preparation, they were the gatekeepers guarding against any male presence.

Stillness and ministrations belonged to Saturday evenings. The charcoal-blue, star-filled night sky watched over mothers, sisters and aunts as they gathered in ritual and retreat to prepare for the Sunday service. Rosters were posted weekly for cleaning and creating flower arrangements. Theirs was a long tradition carried out inside a sacred place, and it constituted a sense of vocation that kept their local church clean, shining and orderly. For the Wellington women, the timeless peace and belonging of the church was their respite from farm duties and unfathomable worries.

Earlier in the day flowers and ferns had been gathered. Joey, Gwen and Adeline already shared in the distinctive language of gardeners and florists. It was early one Saturday evening, twilight time, as the women of the family were getting ready for their rostered church preparation, when Leighton suggested that Joey take Evelyn.

'Evie loves flowers too, Mother. You could show her what happens before the church service.'

'Oh, she'll get too tired.'

'She had an afternoon sleep today,' Leighton retorted.

'I'll look after her. She won't be any bother.' Adeline was always ready for anything.

'She can go to sleep if she needs to. She's never too heavy to carry.' Gwen didn't like Evelyn being left out.

'Well, I guess that's settled then …'

Evelyn joined the devoted and dutiful women as they rejoiced in the beauty and peace of the church – a secret sanctum for sisters. Baskets carried cleaning products and soft polishing rags.

Sisterhood entwined in routine and ritual, with tasks to complete and time together lost inside their own chatter. The vessels and vases were readied for farm flowers, lilac bunches, fresh ferns and branches of lush leaves. Evelyn watched as the mellow light bounced between the women and their work.

Oracles, wise counsel, prophetic predictions, deity inspiration, divine intervention, languages from other worlds; the Wellington sisterhood gathered in the hope of foretelling the future for one of their own, and Evelyn would always be one of them.

A female prophet, my great-grandmother Matilda Wellington had formed well-established insights derived from having eleven children and a quiet husband. She lived by the principles of forgive, forget and forge forward. She was a pioneer of opinionated womanhood and often said, 'God looks after his own.'

Wellington women grew into bestowed roles by design or destiny. Everyone had a place in family folklore. But as often was the case in large families – through biology and assigned roles – the lives of the six Wellington sisters were interwoven.

Joey's eldest sister Phillipa was practical, wise and fuss-free. She attended to what must be done. Joey was energetic, generous and musical – as the third child and second daughter, she was always reliable until self-belief was consumed by self-doubt. Emmeline, the fourth child and third daughter, was creative, gracious and open-hearted. She lived in the world with compassion and wonder. Ethel, gentle, kind and quiet, and the seventh child, faded into the background. The ninth child was May. Opinionated and bold as brass, she usually rubbed her sisters up the wrong way. 'Last Say May' was what their brother Jack called her.

Matilda's seven-year-old niece, Alice, also joined the family when her mother died, a welcome companion for Ida, the eleventh and last Wellington child. The older sisters were navigating grown-up lives when Ida came along.

Wellington women looked after their own and, in their eyes, Joey was in good hands. When they counted their blessings, Evelyn was always included. But Joey questioned whether God had forgotten both her and her daughter of difference.

On Evelyn's first Saturday church evening – her baptism into that intimate theatre of peace, beauty and grace – Auntie Phillipa became another of her guardian angels. There was something about Auntie Phillipa – she appeared to float as she walked. Her hardworking hands held leftover flowers as she approached Evelyn, and made sure she had her attention before speaking.

'Look, Evelyn. Smell these white roses and your mum's lilac. Let's see what you can do with these.'

Strong lilac perfume softened the dusty smell of Queen Anne's lace and asparagus ferns, with their extra feathery foliage that softened the shape of the modest posy that Evelyn and Auntie Phillipa created together.

'Here's a piece of pink ribbon to tie your flowers together,' said Phillipa, as she reached into the large pocket of her calico apron.

Evelyn smiled and completed her task; pride and purpose was something she already understood.

'Clever girl, now you have a beautiful bouquet.'

Joey's daughters always had a place inside Auntie Phillipa's generous heart, for which Joey was forever grateful. Her sisters were reflections of how Joey saw her own place in life, and how she viewed her own mothering. Yet far too often, she would judge herself harshly.

'Oh Philly, I wish I could be more gracious about God testing my faith through Evelyn.'

'Joey, I'll take Evelyn for you tomorrow.' Auntie Phillipa had only ever delivered sons.

'No, Philly. She's better at home with the other children. She seems happier that way.'

Joey's five sisters offered her different things, but two sisters shone more brightly than the others. Phillipa, a healer and a fixer, would listen and move ahead to what could be done. Emmeline was more than a sister to Joey, she was a soulmate. When Emmeline married and moved away to South Africa, letters could never express Joey's loss. And five children in nine years suppressed her emotions faster than the time it took for a letter to reach the postbox, let alone another country. Besides, letters were not the place to complain; love and heartache were part of every woman's story.

When Emmeline moved overseas, communication between the sisters was relegated to birthdays and Christmas. Family ties travelled the oceans and delivered mail that contained good, bad and sad news, but by the time the letters reached their destination, it was always old news. After Evelyn's birth, Joey wanted to confess the story of what she thought had happened to her child. There was no-one else she trusted enough to tell, only Emmeline who lived too far away and had her own children to worry about.

Dusk was the time when Joey watered the garden with thoughts of Emmeline. Time moved on, siblings, parents and spouses passed away. Emmeline lost a child and so did Joey, but they could never fully share in each other's experience; to do so, the sisters needed to be in the same room and the same country.

The absent sister was elevated in family folklore. Over the years, photos of Emmeline's new life turned up along with her letters. Grandmother Wellington and Joey kept them all. Leighton loved the letters his Auntie Emmeline had written, preferring them to the Bible. Throughout his boyhood, he would read them again and again. Leighton would read the letters to Joey at night. For Joey, the empty space of Emmeline's absence was filled by her gentle son.

Although he was still a boy at the time, his awareness of his immediate world and what was missing for people went well beyond his years.

'Mother, do you miss Auntie Emmeline?'

'Every day since she left here, Leighton. Every day.'

'Mother, I would miss Evie if she ever had to go away.'

'Don't even dare to think such a thing! Now, put those letters away, it's bedtime.'

'I hope Evie can read these letters one day.'

'Leighton, you're just like your aunt. You always look on the bright side.'

'I think with Evie, anything is possible.'

'Let's hope that you're right, son.'

6. FAMILY

The dining room was sacrosanct; it was where Sunday lunch took place and it had to be kept spotless. Pride of place was the old Renardi piano valued at £30, worth more than any other piece of household furniture, and a wedding gift to Joey and Arthur from her father, Joseph Wellington. Although Joey did not have the chance to sit at the tapestry stool very often, the piano was her most precious possession. Upon gifting the piano, Joseph had said, 'Joey, your beautiful voice ... never sacrifice a God-given gift like that. Play your piano each day. Find the time for music.'

She had hoped her children would be interested in learning to play. But Gwen and Leighton were the only ones so far who seemed to have any interest or an ear for music. Now and then, someone would lift the lid and let Evelyn plonk away, ever hopeful that it would spark some reaction, other than the tactility of the ivory keys.

Alongside the Renardi was the elegant chiffonier that housed the good crockery and linen. The room held family treasures and furniture that needed polishing. Saturday mornings, Evelyn was included in the sisterly task.

'Rub in circles like this, Lambie,' Gwen instructed.

'Gwennie, look at Evelyn. She is so proud of herself,' Adeline said.

Absorbed in their purposeful polishing, forgotten was what Evelyn could not do.

***

Joey and Arthur spoke in different languages whenever they discussed Evelyn and what was to become of her. In their brief times alone, the early morning extra minutes on the Sabbath before the older children required their attention, Joey would whisper, 'Arthur, I'm worried about Evelyn.'

Delicate puffs of breath would come from the cot at the end of their bed, the soft sounds of Evelyn sleeping.

'Joey, she's perfect. Try not to worry.'

'What's God's plan for Evelyn, and our family?' The question, once stated, could not be taken back.

'I think it's up to us, not God, this time. We can't wait that long,' said Arthur.

'There's something wrong, I just know it.' Joey kept pushing to have her fears heard or dismissed.

'Don't fuss, Joey. It upsets her when you talk like that.'

'But she never knows when we're talking about her.'

'Yes, she does. Especially if she can see your face.'

'Sometimes I don't know what to do …'

'That's enough, now. It's time to get up.'

Arthur was always ready for a new day, but only after he went over to Evelyn's cot to say good morning. Her smile would say it all for him. But that morning, Joey noticed something different about Evelyn.

'Good grief, Arthur! What is she staring at?' she asked, alarmed. Her daughter's focus was usually on her people in the morning.

'The dresser,' replied Arthur, amused.

'Oh, her bouquet. Gwen must have put it there so Evelyn could see it when she woke.' Evelyn had fallen asleep on the way home.

'Don't forget to thank Gwen for being so thoughtful.'

'Arthur, you're not the only one who notices things about our children.'

'How was Evelyn last night at church?'

'She seemed alright. Philly made a fuss of her. She appears to understand the child.'

'Perhaps you should try harder? After all, you're her mother.'

The silence that followed told him to keep his mouth shut. You could go too far with Joey, especially when it concerned Evelyn.

***

Rain, hail or shine, Sunday was not a day of rest. It was morning chores, breakfast, lunch preparation and organising best clothes. After all that was done, Evelyn knew what came next: the horse and buggy would take them to their other world, where the pointy tower poked holes through the ever-shifting sky.

Evelyn, seated in the best position in the house, watched over Sunday rituals. Tucked away inside the orange warmth of the kitchen, she felt safe but also wary. Danger was present: the big, black-bellied stove roared forth in a fury of flames.

'Don't go near the stove, Evelyn,' her mother's mouth would say.

"She won't go near the stove; watch her face. See? She's frightened,' Leighton would reply.

'Well, make sure you keep an eye on her, children.'

Apart from cooking, the stove had other purposes – warming the room, drying clothes and burning old wood. The best thing would happen whenever Joey took out the gravy-stained baking tray. She'd place it on the lower shelf of the stove with a plump leg of mutton, ready for a long, slow cook. The lunchtime roast was the aroma of peace and family seated together every Sunday – same time, same place, same reason.

'Mother, I love everything about Sundays.' Almighty theatre, best clothes, devotion, reflections, observations, kindness and music were what Leighton enjoyed.

'Yes, my boy, I know you do.'

'Look at Evie, she loves watching us coming and going.'

'Well done, Leighton, you always take good care of Evelyn.' Praise from Arthur was rare, and everyone stopped to listen.

What often went unnoticed was Gwen's care. She always dressed Evelyn for church and tied a bow in her sister's hair. This all happened in between milking cows, preparing Sunday lunch and getting herself ready. Everyone knew it was Gwen who loved going to church the most; it was her escape from daily responsibility.

'Gwen? Where are you? Take care of Evelyn. Leighton has to get ready for church.' Joey said this every week. And every week, even with lunchtime chores still to be done, Gwen would dutifully dress her sister.

Leighton noticed, though. He noticed all of his sisters, but he knew Evelyn needed his full attention. He would watch her watching everyone else in the room; she saw everything, including the shape of irritation on Joey's mouth.

'For heaven's sake, Adeline, get something on your feet.' Joey was resigned to the way Adeline did things her own way, but she knew deep down that an independent child was a godsend.

'I don't like wearing shoes.'

'When you're a grown-up, you can wear whatever you like,' Arthur said. He was proud of his barefooted girl, even if she was always trouble coming.

'I certainly will, and don't forget it.'

Uncle Charlie, Arthur's eldest brother, would often say, 'That Adeline Lloyd, you would want her on your side. She'd find a way to win or survive any war.'

'It's not fair, Evelyn should be learning to do more things,' Gwen pointed out.

'Gwen, you know it's too hard to teach her. If you think you can, off you go,' said Joey.

Gwen had watched how Leighton taught Evelyn. Less words, more actions. She determined a new approach was needed.

Mint sauce was the final addition to Sunday lunch, as it made a leg of mutton burst beyond its own flavours. The belief was that the sauce slowed down consumption, allowing for more sheep to be shorn in good and bad seasons.

Gwen picked up a colander and took Evelyn outside to the pot sitting at the back door that overflowed with leafy green mint leaves. She picked some leaves, caught her little sister's eye and said, 'Touch. Smell.'

Evelyn held the leaves to her nose, her tiny fingers stroking the feathery plant. She watched her big sister's words.

'Pick leaves. Put here.' Then Gwen demonstrated. She picked some leaves and placed them in the colander. She gave the container to Evelyn. 'Now, Lambie, you do the same.'

'Lambie' was Gwen's special, secret name for her little sister. No-one else called her that but Gwen.

Gwen watched and waited until she saw Evelyn copy her actions, then went back inside to complete her kitchen chores.

'Where's Evelyn?' Joey asked.

'Outside picking mint leaves for the sauce.'

'Oh for goodness sake, Gwen. She can't do that! It's quicker to do it yourself.'

'Mother, it might be quicker, but she wants to be part of the household.'

'She *is* the blessed household!' Out came Joey's careless words of frustration, fear and failure. 'She's the worry of my life.'

'Please don't say that, Mother. I'm watching her.'

'She'll pick too many stalks. That's extra work.'

'She's happy when she's doing something.'

Soon a triumphant Evelyn stood beneath a halo of doorway sunlight. Pride and purpose held the white colander that was filled to the brim with dark green mint leaves.

'Goodness me, no stalks,' was all Joey could find to say.

'She's taken notice of how we pick the leaves.' Gwen allowed herself the slightest smug tone.

'Words are what I want, Gwennie. Anyone can pick mint leaves,' said Joey, even though this simple gift from Evelyn made her want to cry.

'Good girl,' said Gwen.

To cry in front of others was not the way of Wellington or Lloyd women. If they started, they might never stop and nothing would get done. So Gwen took the mint leaves and transformed them into mint sauce.

Two sets of tight eyes and two firm mouths could not hide their pride from Evelyn, who sensed the body language of her mother's and sister's pain and pleasure. From that day on, mint picking was her job and her contribution to Sunday lunch.

'Not long now, my girl,' Mother said in her softest voice as she opened the back door. 'Play outside, while we finish getting ready for church.'

Evelyn had learned early on not to take up too much space, to wait and watch. Her turn would always come. There was no room for indulged children inside this family. Everyone needed to pull their weight and, on this occasion, so had Evelyn.

7. CHURCH

Not even Sunday could postpone farm chores; cows still needed to be milked, broken fences mended and fractured hearts replenished with faith, hope and charity. Everyone came together to make preparation time run smoothly before church attendance.

There was always a loud voice inside their house of worship. Each week it would announce the same declaration from the pulpit: 'Blessed are the meek, for they will inherit the earth.'

The church's steeple stretched heavenwards to reach beyond the Milawa sky. People prayed for forgiveness, hope, glory and plentiful produce. Sunday in the stony churchyard was the gathering place for faithful followers from local farming families. Transport was haphazard, with horses, carts, bicycles or people's God-given feet. Matilda and Joseph Wellington were two of the few who arrived in the latest contraption – a car. The older children rode a horse, two or three astride, or squeezed themselves onto a buggy trailer. Little ones, like Evelyn, sat in the cart with their parents. Dusty boots were wiped clean at the church gates, and inside the Ten Commandments were waiting to be followed. The Wellington family also had an

Eleventh Commandment: cleanliness of mind, body and language.

Before she entered the four walls of gilded light, Evelyn would watch through the arched doorway and observe soft rays of individual rainbows fall across the chapel from inside a prism of sunlight. Stained-glass windows invited the shadows of unknown prophets to stroll beneath glowing shapes of colour. Evelyn – bright-eyed, wide-eyed and a wordless witness – moved through the doors and crossed between her two worlds of home and church.

A children's nursery rhyme that all of the Lloyd children knew combined talking on hands, visual learning and imagination. It was a sing-song poem that reinforced church culture and the saying of prayers:

Here's the church and here's the steeple,
Open the door and see all the people.
Here's the parson going upstairs,
And here he is, he's saying his prayers.

Leighton had tried to teach this poem to Evelyn. She would follow his hand movements, but he realised they meant little to her without the story. Leighton knew never to confuse his sister with too much information, so he did not push her.

At Milawa, there was a church, a red-brick steeple, arched doors and all her people. Evelyn could see the minister going up the stairs and saw him shape his prayers. When the time came for heads to be bent in meditative contemplation or prayer, Evelyn's tiny fingers traced the soft texture of the silk bow that Gwen had tied in her hair.

Gwen had said, 'Pretty Lambie.' But Evelyn never knew that the white lamb in the stained-glass windows she was staring at was also her sister's pet name for her.

Sheltered in her father's arms inside a mist of golden light, Evelyn saw in his form her own God, her own hero – a towering pillar of sight, smell, touch and understanding.

To Arthur, Evelyn was an unexpected voice of reason, reflection and restoration. Yet he knew that finding language for Evelyn would require a sacrifice beyond love and prayers. Education for Evelyn was not going to fall from heaven.

In the Oxley Shire community, most children learned to read, write, pray and work hard. All the Lloyd children attended the Hurdle Creek West State School, at least when chores and weather did not intervene. Although not one family member put words to the thought, everyone sensed that Evelyn would not be joining her siblings at the local school.

In church, Evelyn would sit on her father's knee with Leighton seated beside them. Parishioners did not have a chance against the two children skim-reading the congregation; Evelyn and Leighton could see it all. Mother always stood front and centre of the choir, and Gwen was in the second row. The other siblings would be seated with cousins closer to the front of the church, parents too far away to reprimand any bad behaviour, although country children always knew what was expected from them.

***

Church was a meeting place for prayers and gossip shared on the same doorstep. You never knew what would happen next, even in this tiny church where most people were related or knew each other. There was that Sunday when Joey's sister May made an entrance that interrupted the singing of the opening hymn:

Let it shine on me, let it shine on me,
Oh, let Your light from the lighthouse shine on ...

And shine it did – on the sly stares and shuffling spaces as the light shifted into a sinister silence and the singing seemed to stop. May Nichols (nee Wellington), poised in her best feathered hat and with the sharp eyes of a homing pigeon, surveyed each wooden pew. When Auntie May spied a seat, she raised her gloved claw and waved. Her intention was clear as her ruffled shoulders swooped past puzzled parishioners. A moment later, she plonked herself right beside her sister's husband and said, 'Well, what do you know, Arthur? A spare seat!' And with a voice as loud as hers, most people heard every word.

Not quite speechless, there was nowhere for Arthur to look. Church or not, he could not turn the other cheek. But at least the singing kept going.

'Hello, May,' he whispered.

It had been said more than once that May had more front than Myers.

'Oh, Arthur, I know it's a bit of a squish, but there's just enough room for me here ... right beside you.' May could mark her territory in a way her sisters would never dare.

Although she was like a bad penny that always turned up, when she was finally seated, Auntie May was forgotten for the moment. Another performer was preparing a change of scene in this Sunday matinee. The stage was set, and the audience willing. Evelyn watched the organist, a straight-backed farmer's wife, seated in pride of place beside her own importance. Her laced-up best shoes suspended on brass pedals, she stretched her strong fingers and held the moment, the congregation and Evelyn in her thrall. Taking deep breaths and raising her proud chin, she pulled out organ stops in the same way she milked a cow. Her solid shoulders shifted to a slow beat, her fingers teased, caressed and seduced the keys of the organ. It was a delicious moment for Mrs Jones.

The unusual construction of tiered flat black-and-white keyboards with round knobs was another nameless Sunday object of shape and colour. It reminded Evelyn of the big black stove at home. Evelyn had learned that everything had two sides – the stove was frightening, but kept the family warm and well fed. In church, the organ's heavy vibrations that came up through the floor were less intimidating when she could see what would happen next.

Mrs Jones banged the keys, pulled out all the stops and played with passionate purpose as the shiny black-green feathers on her hat fluttered with her movement. The organist was one miracle worth seeing. Evelyn wanted to tell Leighton, Father and Cliff to watch for the sunlit clouds of powder rising from the cheeks of the warrior woman; she knew they would see the funny side.

Evelyn had seen women dust their faces with the velvety, soft powder of grown-up glamour. One day on a visit to Auntie May's, while the adults were talking, eating homemade cake and drinking tea, Leighton had held Evelyn's hand and pointed his finger to pursed lips. Then they had stepped lightly away from the gathering and crept down the dark passageway, where the smell of furniture polish and lily-of-the-valley greeted them. Leighton always knew where he was going, and soon they had located Auntie May's bedroom.

There, just ahead, was the elegance of a mahogany dressing table with a lace doily, a silver filigreed mirror, a brush and comb set, a crystal bowl with a silver lid holding pale pink powder and a soft fluff like a dandelion. May used this bowl to keep herself attractive to men. Joey had no time for powdering her face, and Gwen and Adeline were still too young for vanity.

Every space of the forbidden room was filled with powdery perfumes of soft musk, violet, rose, daphne, lavender and lilac. The fragrances disturbed Evelyn, but Leighton lifted the lid on Auntie May's crystal container without hesitation. A moment later, she sensed texture and perfume from the rosy powder puff as her brother placed soft smudges on both their faces, then shy smiles and playful eyes reflected back at them in the mirror. A clean hanky swiped the evidence away before anyone caught them. In any case, Leighton would always take the blame for leading her astray.

Hearing footsteps, Leighton grabbed Evelyn's hand and they ran outside, quickly disappearing beneath the safe green hands of the big-leafed fig tree. They flopped onto the ground and giggled at their own daring. Leighton put his hands together in the prayer position, then opened out his hands. He banged away as if playing on the church organ, then flicked his hands away from his cheeks, reminding Evelyn of the organist's performance in the language they shared.

8. AUNTIE MAY

There was a reason for May's behaviour, but never an excuse. Her sensible sisters would only let her go so far. 'There are many virtues, but following your own desires is not one of them,' Phillipa would say.

Sisters like Phillipa turned up when they were needed. Others, like May, overstepped the mark. Out visiting, at church or at home, nobody could escape Auntie May's opinions, especially about Evelyn. Leighton heard her say more than once, 'There's something odd about that child. And the way they all pander to her! Even Arthur, who should know better.'

She knew when to pick her moment. Leighton noticed she was always careful about what she said in front of his father.

'Joey, those children of yours are spoiled rotten.' May would keep going with badly timed and unwanted guidance. 'If you want my advice, you're making a rod for your own back.'

'May, I don't think you understand children.'

'Of course I do! Spoiling them is not the way.'

'That's what you think.'

When May asked, 'Whatever is wrong with that child?',

Evelyn saw her aunt's face transform into the shape of a cat. But whenever Arthur was in the room, May's face would slide back into the shape of a doting aunt.

Leighton would hear Auntie May say, 'Dear little Evelyn, come and sit on my knee,' but Evelyn couldn't be fooled. To Leighton's relief, his sister would stand back and remain safely out of May's reach. Evelyn never willingly went to her, not the way she would happily run into the open arms of her beloved Auntie Phillipa.

'That May, she'd try the patience of a saint,' said Joey, to cover her own unease at May's behaviour.

The truth was an un-Christian thought. It was clear to others that Arthur was not oblivious to May's charms. Grandmother Wellington often said that May was a force unto herself, and she understood her son-in-law was a charmer who liked women, the prettier the better. While he was always faithful to Joey, his head could easily be turned. May was a formidable woman still finding her way, and she wanted attention. But it was hard on Joey that May's need came at a time when she was busy coming to terms with 'what's wrong with Evelyn?'. All Joey needed was a quiet moment to accept her circumstances and her youngest daughter, without any of May's mischief to distract her.

Compassion was the country way, and her sisters tried. A brief step into motherhood for May was buried with the passing of her baby boy, one-month-old Alan, who rested with his father Vic at Milawa Cemetery. Both a child and a husband lost within a year of each other. Forgiveness of May's behaviour was easier for Matilda. She remembered the day of the life-threatening birth and when the doctor whispered to her, 'May will never carry another baby. She's fortunate to be alive to tell this tale.'

In a fertile family, this was May's cross to bear. It was hard to ignore or forget how all the Wellington women had produced numerous children, except for May.

There was a Twelfth Commandment that could have been written for Wellington women: 'Thou shalt not put your emotions on display.' They followed the Commandments and believed 'Thy will be done on earth, as it is in heaven.' Only May was not so sure about heaven; she was on earth and her will would be done her way.

'Arthur, watch out for May,' cautioned Joey.

'May's been through a lot,' he replied.

'Haven't we all?'

'Look at what you have, Joey.'

'Yes, Arthur. Responsibility, and not one excuse that anyone cares about.'

Joey told me more than once the story of how Arthur gave May a box of embroidered handkerchiefs for her birthday. He had forgotten Joey's birthday in January earlier that same year, the one where she was pregnant again, and was coming to terms with the crushing diagnosis for Evelyn. The details were still clear, and so was her resentment.

Over forty years had passed when my grandmother first told me this story about May; I understood that my grandfather's actions had never been forgotten or forgiven by her. Every good family story has a villain, but a femme fatale in country Victoria seemed even more exotic to me, and I was happy to claim Auntie May as ours.

9. CHANGE IS COMING

Worry had to step aside for changes in the weather, the toughest taskmaster. Winter days were floods and animals stuck in the creek. Every family member had to muck in, except those too small to get behind a cow and push it from the mud.

Adeline, still a small child herself, watched over Evelyn while the others were in the fields. She pointed and said, 'Wait here at the back door, Evelyn, where you can see me peeling the veggies for dinner. And you can watch the rain, too.'

The Bobinawarrah sky was covered with bundles of scowling clouds, weeping silver-aqua water across the soggy paddocks. Evelyn's pert nose tilted skywards as she breathed in the rising smell of grassy, muddy rain. She stared through the wispy blue-grey mist into the distance, until she recognised the shapes and gait of her people coming back home through the haze.

Seeing them return, Adeline went back inside, stood on a chair and filled the old iron kettle, readying it for someone bigger to carry it across to the stove. Through the doorway, smelling of mud, cows, damp clothing and tiredness, came Evelyn's people, one by one.

'Up you come, Evelyn,' Arthur called. 'Was Evelyn a good girl for you, Adeline?'

'Yes, Father, but she wouldn't leave the back door until you all returned.'

'Thank you for filling the kettle and looking after your sister. Down now, Evelyn, while I change into some dry clothes.' Evelyn sat back on her chair, content to watch her people move into the patterns, rhythms and shapes of evening-meal preparation.

Parents would never explain life to themselves or their children. Telling lies was a sin, but nothing said meant nothing lost, gained or confronted. However, the time was coming to face the truth: Arthur wanted a voice for his child.

Whenever Arthur watched Evelyn, he felt a return to things long forgotten: wonder, hope and the innocence of joy. Her curious hands touched surfaces, traced shapes, twisted fabrics; he knew that her fingers were discovering meaning. And there was only so long before decisions would have to be made and followed through.

Evelyn's strange, soft sounds, her unexplainable knowing and how the simplest words, like 'Mumma' and 'Dadda', were never said unsettled Joey. The family embraced Evelyn's difference, but her mother was always worried about what other people thought.

'Who cares, Joey? That's not our concern. Our only concern is Evelyn. Don't forget that.'

'Arthur, you can be very sure that is the one thing I will never forget.'

'What is it, then?'

'She will have to go away.' There was no retracting the fear within her words.

'Mother, don't talk like that about Evie where she can see your face. It frightens her.' Leighton was ever mindful, but his mother ignored him.

'You think you know everything, Leighton, but you don't,' Gwen said, wanting to avoid the inevitable truths that were coming.

'At least I know that—'

'Enough, children. You mustn't argue in front of Evelyn,' Arthur said, bringing the discussion under control. Gwen and Leighton stopped at once; their father's voice held the final say.

Evelyn watched. While she had no words of identification for her parents and siblings, each face held a place of certainty in her world. The face of worry was Mother, Father had the face of acceptance, Cliff the face of irrepressible fun, Gwen the face of sacrifice and responsibility, Leighton had the face of charm and connection, Adeline the face of resilience. When baby Evan arrived, his was a face of gentle observation.

Evelyn knew more about her people than they could ever realise.

A spatial learner, she scanned eyes, foreheads, chins, mouths, hands; every body part had a way of speaking to her. Puzzled faces were always trying to peer into her thoughts. They all wanted to understand, but when faces closed or turned away they told Evelyn there was something different about her, something wrong.

People were unsure what to call her difference. Except for Cousin Vaughan. 'I don't think Evelyn can hear anyone.'

His honest assessment of his cousin was more than some members in the family were ready to acknowledge.

***

Country doctors – some gentle, some rough – examined Evelyn. There had been horse and buggy rides into town. Behind surgery doors, Evelyn breathed in the mixed medicinal smells that carried warning signs of unexplainable intrusion. Doctors with smooth, firm hands had touches she did not trust. And then there was Dr W. Browne. His thick, bushy moustache covered his words – it was the very reason Arthur kept his face whisker-free.

The Wangaratta doctor tapped her back and chest, firm and steady, looked down her throat, poked a yellow light inside both ears and banged his hands together far too close to her head. Evelyn was anxious around the strange man. His hands needed to be watched.

For Joey, the words 'retarded' and 'dumb' were difficult to accept from the family doctor. The time had come to silence uninformed guesses; something else was needed. She knew that a big-city specialist would have the answer, even if it was one that she did not want to hear.

At dinner, Joey announced what the next day would bring.

'Children, I'm taking Evelyn to Melbourne to see a specialist. Grandfather will take us to the train station.'

'Can I come too, to keep Evelyn company?'

'Not this time, Adeline. You need to help Gwen take care of things here.'

'Auntie Phillipa can help her. I don't trust those doctors with Evelyn.' Adeline was protective of her little sister.

'That's enough, Miss. I'll be looking after her.'

'Make sure you watch her all the time,' said Adeline, resolute.

Arthur had the final say. 'Enough, Adeline. Your mother will take good care of our little one.'

They had all begun to sense Evelyn's growing distraction and disconnect, but it was the not-knowing that caused Joey distress. The future of this family was a storm coming that no-one could prepare for.

***

From when I was around the age of seven, people would frequently ask me why my mother was born the way she was. Evelyn was my mother and I didn't want another one, but the question reinforced to me that she was different, that there was something 'wrong' with her. And there was only one person I could ask.

My grandmother told me that when she was pregnant with Evelyn, she became unwell and had to go to hospital for two weeks. It was her fifth full-term pregnancy, and Evelyn was her first and only child to be delivered in a hospital. Nurse Parker delivered Evelyn Ida Lloyd on 30 March 1917. There was no doctor in attendance.

When baby Evelyn would not breastfeed, the nurse came into the room and shook her to make her take the breast. I asked Joey many times what she did when that happened. Every time, her reply left me feeling sad for both of them.

'I was so upset that I didn't know what to do.'

Sometimes it is too late to speak up about something you don't know how to fix. It was the story that Joey had wanted to confess to Emmeline, but couldn't.

When I was older, I asked Joey if she might have had German measles, one of the main possible causes of my mother's difference.

'I could have done. I would never have known … I was just too busy with everyday life.'

10. A JOURNEY BEGINS

My great-grandfather, Joseph Wellington, was an important man in Joey's life. He was born in 1852 in La Ville Périac, France, but his parents soon took him back to their hometown of St Buryan, Cornwall, in England. When he was five years old, the extended Wellington family undertook the hazardous ship journey to Australia. As an adult, he settled in the Oxley Shire and fathered eleven children.

Grandfather Wellington was a reserved man, but his daughter Josephine, who shared the female derivative of his name, seemed to understand her father's quiet ways. He was old and thin. His hair and pointy beard were the colour of snow on the mountains and his face was like crinkled paper. His stooped body formed the shape of a letter that Evelyn had seen but didn't yet know: the letter S.

Matilda Wellington and her daughters stepped in and out of their different roles of helping Joey come to terms with Evelyn. Overwhelmed by bustling womanhood, her father only had his patient, practical and physical support to offer.

Grandfather Wellington had a car, rare for country people at that time, and on Joey and Evelyn's significant day, he drove them to Wangaratta Station. A small child separated from a place of belonging with nothing explained was an unspoken but familiar part of his own experience.

On the day of Evelyn's appointment in Melbourne, Joey buttoned her anxiety beneath her best coat and prayed that her courage would not come apart at the seams, at least not until after she and Evelyn had boarded the train. The rare luxury of being driven by car to the station was not enough to divert the future of Joey's family.

The task of attending the specialist's appointment had fallen to Joey; Arthur had not been ready for this stage of Evelyn's journey and cited farm work as an excuse. Life had not turned out as Joey had expected. At thirty-eight, she was too young for any more disappointments and felt far too old for any more surprises.

Evelyn understood that suitcases meant a trip. No suitcase for Grandfather Wellington meant that he was not travelling with them. The brown leather case told her the story – she and Mother were the only ones catching the train.

Evelyn could see her mother's hardworking hands and noticed that she was wearing her pretty ring, the one for special occasions. Four small white stones and the two bigger red rubies sparkled with silver stars of light, but the worn gold of the wedding ring told another story.

The ground beneath Evelyn's feet shifted like schools of fish swimming through the Ovens River. What confused some of her family was when she would jump to certain household noises and vibrations, as if she had heard them instead of felt them.

Waiting on the platform, Evelyn sensed that her mother, who was also wearing her pretty brooch clasped at her throat, was like a pile of washing ready to tumble over and scatter everywhere.

Joey tried hard to ignore the quizzical stare and soft sounds that came from Evelyn. She looked around to see if others could hear those strange noises, worried they might misinterpret her four-year-old's intellect. Her and Arthur's families were well known in the district and Joey had one main fear: of being judged and found wanting as a mother.

'Escaping milking is the only good thing about this trip,' she said to her father. But there was someone else who did not seem to hear Joey – Grandfather Wellington was going deaf.

The tickets had been booked and paid for by Grandfather Wellington – first class to Melbourne in the Ladies' Compartment meant well-sprung maroon leather seats, privacy, comfort and convenience. Joey and Evelyn would be close to the lavatories and buffet car for the long trip.

Trepidation for Joey was leaving behind her other children, her husband's commitment and the support of her Lloyd and Wellington kinfolk. On this journey, she would be alone with her child of difference. Finding any time alone with Evelyn was difficult, and now here they were, not knowing what would happen next.

While Joey had staying power in spades, some days it did go missing. Everyone, even God, seemed to be going deaf, although Joey would never say that to her own father. It would break his heart to hear Joey doubting God. Still, hearts always got broken and, on this trip, Joey knew it was her turn. Any diagnosis for Evelyn would reinforce Joey's greatest fear: her little daughter would have to leave the farm and her family.

The black-capped station master called, 'All aboard, all aboard … ALL ABOARD!', his words scattering across station sounds. Time was closing in on final goodbyes and future outcomes. They boarded the train.

Joey had the train window down, trying to find the words to thank her father for all he had done for her.

'Father, I don't know what to …'

'Shush, all will be well.'

'I wish that were true.'

'Joey, it's all for Evelyn.'

'Father, what if they—'

The high-pitched despair in Joey's whispered words was swallowed by the sound of steam coming from the engine.

'Never, Joey. Never.'

Futures could change in the blink of an eye and Joseph Wellington appreciated how ships, trains and destinies waited for no-one. When they had been standing on the station platform, her father had taken Joey's hand and pressed some money across her palm. Her fingers had closed firmly around it. Extra for the Melbourne trip, the doctor and impending outcomes. Her pride pocketed, Joey was grateful and hoped for a quiet moment to reflect upon the grace of God and her own father. He bent down to look into the face of his grandchild, opened his timeworn hand and waited for her to do the same. He gifted a silver coin into Evelyn's open palm, then closed her hand around the shiny, bumpy, still-warm button.

I believe he understood why people were unsure when they interacted with Evelyn. She received more presents than the other children because it was the only language some people could find. But he also believed language was one of God's many gifts that would find Evelyn when the time was right.

The train shuddered in anticipation. Evelyn traced the fine ridges of her new gift, a disc on which a man wore something on his head; not a hat, but a crown. The other side had two tall animals. One of them, she had seen many times before. It had a small head, a large body, a long tail and hopped past the farm on two big legs. It had grey paws like branches that kept it from falling over. But she had never seen the other one. It looked like a bird too large to fly.

Grandfather Wellington wanted to tell this treasured child how his son Charlie had been born blind and had attended the Royal Victorian Institute for the Blind in Melbourne. The shared common language of instruction, music and prayer united Charlie with his family, although none of these languages seemed to belong in Evelyn's world. Instead, he said a silent prayer for his daughter Joey. He hoped she would find her own path of faith, acceptance and a language she could share with Evelyn.

Joey once told me about her father taking them to the station, and my imagination revisits his ancestral stoicism as this part of my history stood on the station and waved his daughter and granddaughter towards a distant diagnosis. Life cycles never stop, and I wonder if he paused to consider how his own grandfather might have felt, waving goodbye to loved ones, never knowing if he would ever see them again as they sailed towards the dreams and dilemmas that would take place on foreign soil.

Evelyn and Joey had a window seat. Train trips were a rarity. Joey would never allow her children to stand on train seats but, as Evelyn was too small to see out, she made an allowance. There would be a lot to see: people passing in the passageway, big skies, treetops, buildings, bridges, rivers and stations soaring past.

Nobody knew what could disturb Evelyn's balance – the banging of a door, thunder and now the tremor of the train all through her body. The black-hatted conductor marched up and down clipping tickets, and a taller uniformed man leaned outside the train, red-cheeked and cheery-faced from blowing into a silver whistle. Suddenly, the stout and sturdy engine shuddered as they were wrenched away from the station.

Evelyn's grandfather waited on the platform until the train pulled out of sight.

11. MOTHERHOOD

As the train pulled away from the station, Joey sank into the sumptuous seats and started the journey into her own thoughts. Resolutions and reality were set aside until the appointment with the specialist.

Joey had a secret. Her belief was fragile, but hope deserved one final shot: she planned to visit a psychic in St Kilda. For her, acceptance of Evelyn's difference was taking too long. She needed an answer, and any answer would do to stop her blaming herself.

After a lullaby of steady rocking, Evelyn fell sound asleep. Joey looked at her daughter. The dear little girl was not to blame. Instead, Joey held herself responsible. She had been the one to ignore the tell-tale signs of difference in Evelyn. As the train gathered speed, so did her thoughts.

With Evelyn's head weightless on her lap, Joey's softer thoughts travelled well beyond the train window. Everybody had been part of the early-morning start, but now here she was with time to herself. Her thoughts returned to her many pregnancies. She still saw her children as moments of perfection, and now she had another child on the way, due in April.

Alone with her unborn baby and her greatest fear, Joey

pondered what would happen if her new child turned out like Evelyn. It would be one gift too many, but they would have to manage somehow. Joey was in need of rest and respite in order to quell the frustration she still felt in the years after her youngest daughter's birth in a hospital. Again and again, Joey would think back to the rough nurse, shaking her new baby because she would not breastfeed. She needed to believe in a certain truth so she could keep moving forward. While a case of German measles could have been the cause, neither option could change the past or ease her anxiety.

Her children always inundated her thoughts. She worried about them in different ways. She had overheard her own mother say, 'That Cliff's a little tartar. He needs a firmer hand.' She knew his lightheartedness might not be right for leading their family, but he brought her much-needed joy.

Arthur would express his frustrations about Cliff, saying, 'That boy thinks life is playing football, riding horses and knocking around with his cousins.'

'He's only a boy and he likes having fun.'

'Fun! There's more to life than fun.'

Arthur was also a country boy and, to be fair, he'd had his share of fun, freedom and glory. No-one ever mentioned within his earshot how Cliff's birth had happened only seven months after Arthur and Joey were married. Arthur, as the third-born son, had dodged the heavy expectations that belonged to his two older brothers. His father, one of the historical 'Farmers Five', had passed his prospects and the family's historic homestead, Tarramia, on to Arthur's eldest brother.

Life had rushed at Joey; Gwen was born only eighteen months after Cliff. Gwen was a hard worker and a dedicated big sister. Joey was aware that having a sibling who was different created a sense of responsibility that was too much for a young girl. But there was nothing Joey could do about it but notice and revisit the words her mother would say, 'God looks after his own, so he will look after our Gwen.'

Joey did not mean to have a favourite child. She had a soft spot for Cliff, but Leighton was her God-given gift. Her intuitive third child filled the empty space left by Emmeline's absence. Wise beyond his years, he understood her feelings and she never felt judged by him. Grandmother Wellington often warned Joey not to be too dependent on him. 'He's still only a boy,' she reminded her. But Joey couldn't stop herself from turning to the open-hearted and available support he offered.

Adeline, only three years older than Evelyn, was centred, social and strong. But more often than not, attention was diverted away from Adeline, with the family focus on the male heirs and Evelyn. Encouragement was a foreign language for country girls. Grandmother Wellington noticed this and said, 'Anything's possible for that Adeline Lloyd, I just hope she gets her chance.'

Both older girls had the promise, strength, courage and commitment needed to take the Lloyd family name and farm forward. Yet Arthur Lloyd accepted without question that female futures were limited in choice and opportunity. His last will and testament rewarded the males for their gender, not their contribution. This was one family value

Joey and her daughters found hard to accept. Each of my aunts would tell me this same story in their own way, and more than once.

All of Joey's children were individual in their own way, just as any mother would want. They were kind, loyal and diligent, and they all loved Evelyn. What was overlooked at the time was how young they all were to be taking on so much responsibility. But some burdens were too heavy to carry alone. Joey needed her children to make sense of what was yet to come, and she was not the first mother to ask too much of her children and of herself, nor would she be the last.

The train's steady rhythm also allowed Joey time to contemplate the new baby growing inside her. She permitted herself to dream of another son. Boys were easier, and potential farmers; the future of their property would be in good hands with another boy.

She remembered the words her mother had said before the trip: 'Joey, count your blessings. There's no reason why another baby will not be as perfect in its own way, as is Evelyn.'

Be that as it may, there was one thing Joey knew for sure – she would not be giving birth in hospital.

As the world raced by and Evelyn slept on, Joey turned her thoughts to a name for her new baby. This time, Arthur would allow Joey to choose, and she wanted family history to be acknowledged. 'Emmeline Anne' if it was a girl, after her sister and Arthur's mother, or the proud Welsh name 'Evan Westall' for a boy, to honour Arthur's father, Charles Westall Lloyd.

Although she feared having another child of difference, what didn't occur to Joey on that trip was what it would be like for Evelyn to have a sibling like herself – someone to share her language, be a playmate and understand things from that particular point of view.

12. CITY VISIT

Melbourne was where trams the colour of green tree frogs trundled past looking important and convenient, each one packed with people going places. Evelyn could feel the tremor of the tram through the soles of her leather boots just before it stopped for her and her mother.

Joey lifted her onto the wooden running board. Through the open doorway was the wide road filled with horses, carts, cars, bicycles and even a motorbike. The tram stopped and started outside wide-fronted shops and grand buildings where Joey and Evelyn saw city women wearing coats with big fur collars. Joey slipped back to a time of shopping with Emmeline and buying coats that reflected style, not practicality and Sundays.

Dressed in their Sunday best, she and Evelyn watched as country and city lives merged into the traffic. New surprises, unforeseen futures – no-one around them knew they were headed to the specialist located on the corner of Collins and Spring streets. Trees, tall buildings, churches, shops and offices rushed past. Then the conductor called their tram stop and Joey stood steadfast, holding Evelyn tight.

'Thy will be done,' Joey sighed to herself.

Dark room, dark furniture. Dark shadows from paper-brown trees swayed outside the tall window. They were upstairs, inside the luxurious office and medical room. The specialist – a well-dressed and tubby man – poked at Evelyn, but all the while looked at Joey. His lips moved into sharp shapes for the final diagnosis: 'profoundly deaf' … 'deaf and dumb' … 'institution'.

Simple words that struck with the precision of a butcher's knife.

Evelyn had witnessed death on the farm, and she sensed a similar feeling in the room. Mother gazed into her lap, as shock slowly shredded the fine lace on the corners of her best linen handkerchief.

The plush room was scary and somehow sad; they needed to escape. Evelyn held her mother's hand as they went down the stairs and outside into the sunshine, neither of them able to appreciate being at the Paris end of Collins Street, amid all that style and elegance. For now, they were two fugitives needing to step back onto a tram, step off at the big station and step onto the long train which would take them home where they belonged.

Joey had wanted to ask the specialist another question, but she hadn't been able to find the words to ask whether her new baby would also be born 'deaf and dumb'. One problem at a time was enough for today.

***

Contradictions were a hearing mother and a deaf child, and Christianity and spiritualism. The psychic was Joey's last hope, but one she would not share with her family.

Good fortune was that Evelyn could never tell; Arthur would never have agreed to such hocus pocus.

Joey and Evelyn boarded a tram that took them to St Kilda, and Joey looked the other way when they passed the Victorian Deaf and Dumb Institution.

St Kilda's residents in the 1920s fluctuated between the gentry, Jewish immigrants, entertainers, prostitutes, criminals and the various roustabouts found at boarding houses. A melting pot containing people of every shape, size and class. When their tram stopped on bustling St Kilda Road, Evelyn was shocked by what she could see: water, much bluer and bigger than her rivers at home, and ahead, something even stranger.

She was not sure which way to look. Flags flew from the tops of two red, pink and blue pillars; a huge white moon face loomed over her with raised eyebrows, sly eyes, a furious frown, scrunched cheeks, an arch of bright red lips and big ugly teeth. More people materialised, only to disappear inside the mouth-cave. Above the entrance face, she could see white, wooden-framed mountains on which buckets of people went down and up, down and up. Evelyn had never seen anything like this before.

Heading away from the main activity, Joey was resolute. They went down a godforsaken street, then a cobbled laneway filled with old food smells, until they reached a rough and ready staircase leading to a broken door. There had already been too many stairs for one day. Arriving at the landing, they pushed through the dreary door that opened into a strange room.

Once inside and seated, Joey could see that Breda, the

clairvoyant, was of an indeterminate age and had a strong Irish accent that was hard to follow. She asked to hold Joey's ruby ring in her hand and said, 'God be with you, as we cross to the other world.' Reluctantly, Joey handed the ring over. Her belief wavered when every voice from the other side came back in the woman's broad Irish accent. At the very least, Joey had expected ancestral Welsh or Cornish voices to turn up and guide her.

Suddenly, she was too overwhelmed to listen. Neither clairvoyance nor Christianity could ease her fractured heart or provide a resolution for her troubles. Embarrassed, money squandered, Joey's hopes for a different outcome were dashed. There was no alternative future – Evelyn was 'deaf and dumb'. Whatever was said from then on, that diagnosis would never change.

Stunned, Joey needed to escape yet another stifling room. Of course, she remembered to ask for her ring back; that was one story she did not want to explain.

Feeling foolish, Joey had just enough dignity left to board a tram to Camberwell where they would stay overnight with Arthur's sister. Auntie Ethel had an evening meal waiting, that they accepted gratefully; lunch had been forgotten.

Even from a distance, Evelyn recognised Auntie Ethel's way of walking. It was clear she belonged to Father. Their skin colouring, brown hair, kind eyes and even their ears were similar. They were Evelyn's people, and she would know them anywhere.

The day did have some moments of good fortune: open arms had welcomed them, and cousin Connie had knitted

Evelyn a cardigan of red wool. And in the morning they would be travelling back home in first class, thanks to Grandfather Wellington.

***

Instead of daydreams, reality chaperoned Joey on the return trip. Losing one of her children to Melbourne was one 'gift' she did not want to accept from God, or anyone else for that matter. Joey wanted to make peace with God, but somewhere deep inside her being making peace with herself had to come first.

Now that she had an official name for Evelyn's difference, the future was confirmed. The only consolation was the possibility of Leighton taking up a teaching career in the future. If he was teaching in Melbourne, he could be close to Evelyn and continue to watch over her.

The train was warm. Evelyn, overindulged, overstimulated and over-prodded, sat beside Joey. She stroked the soft wool of her new red cardigan, lost inside her own thoughts of the fast-flowing city, the many staircases and strange people. The best part had been staying overnight with her Dixon cousins in the big brick house.

Joey was also lost in thought. She did not notice the way Evelyn held her nose to block the dirty smell of coal, or that her leather boots did not reach the floor. Also unheeded was the small coat hanging on the brass rack, and how her child's tiny fingers traced known and unknown textures.

Soon they reached Seymour Station, the stopover for hot lunches, sandwiches, fruitcake and cups of tea. Beyond their first-class carriage, the platform was overflowing with life.

Well-behaved people hurried past the wide window on their way to the station's cafeteria, but Joey stayed put. She would rather go hungry than have to talk to anyone on this return trip. Instead, they took a seat in the elegant dining car. Evelyn sat on a red velvet cushion. The white starched tablecloth was stiff to touch; she took extra care not to spill her milk. Joey stared straight ahead and sipped her tea from the bone china cup with its gold rim and matching saucer.

Back inside their carriage and on their way again, the countryside started to look familiar and Evelyn knew she was nearly home. Joey took their suitcase and coats down from the brass rack and placed them on the seat. Evelyn slid her hand inside the soft, white satin pocket of her warm coat and stretched her fingers across the smooth roundness of Grandfather Wellington's gift. The coin was still there and, for that moment at least, everything else was in its place too.

As the train reached the platform, Evelyn saw Father waving. She waved back to him, or perhaps it was to her own reflection in the window.

Buttoned up in their Sunday coats, Joey and Evelyn looked much the same as when they had left home. Standing on the platform with Arthur, difference was not easy to detect.

'Up you come, Evelyn.' And she was safely back in her father's arms where she belonged.

On the way home, she sat in the buggy sandwiched between her parents. Joey's tired silence told Arthur all he needed to know: Evelyn's diagnosis meant their little girl would be leaving her home, her community and her family, which was a discussion to be had after the children went to bed.

The silence gave Arthur time to ponder the future. He did not know how he was going to trust Evelyn to others. He wanted to be available always when Evelyn made the transition between two worlds.

13. THE TRUTH

Before sunrise, the cranky rooster reminded the family that it was the start of a new day. Joey was tired, heavy and sick with worry. Like winter rain, bad news never seemed to stop: first Arthur, and now Evelyn.

Arthur had shown signs of illness for some years. Twelve months before Evelyn's diagnosis, his tiredness and pain had finally been given a name: Bright's disease, a serious and then-incurable kidney disorder. No-one dared to say how long he had to live, and some felt it was best not to know. One thing Arthur and Joey had agreed upon was to take each day as it came.

Now they would have to do the same with Evelyn.

The kitchen was alive and the children wary. They knew any news from Melbourne would have to wait until the evening meal. Evelyn was the only one unscathed from the last few days – her life had returned to family attention and farm adventures.

Although she usually slept in her parents' room, the previous night she had shared her big sisters' bed in preparation for when the new baby arrived. Her cot would then be moved into a three-sister bedroom. Neither Joey nor Arthur were ready to have her move away from them, but that night they needed to talk, despite knowing that Evelyn would not hear one word.

The night his mother and sister had arrived home, after everyone was in bed, Leighton had placed himself on the other side of his parents' closed bedroom door. He overheard his father's fall from grace: this farming man could not save Evelyn from being sent away, nor could he mend Joey's broken heart.

Arthur was considered a local war hero, although Leighton was unsure about the way war defined heroes. To him, his father was an ordinary man with everyday faults who would often sneak away to the Milawa pub and return home smelling of alcohol. Joey would be cross and Gwen embarrassed, but everyone else enjoyed Father's good humour on those nights.

Listening, Leighton understood that fateful decisions were taking place. Then the boy heard something he wished to never know.

'He wants her to go to the Victorian Deaf and Dumb Institution, Arthur. My child, put away in an institution? Over my dead body!'

'Joey, it's what we have to do.'

Leighton was nearly eleven at that time. He already knew his Evie was deaf, that she learned differently. The word 'dumb' was more difficult to accept. But the word that scared him was 'institution'.

Differences in society were not explained; being shut away and separated from loved ones seemed to be the only solution. Country life isolated Leighton from understanding how institutions functioned, but the most important thing for him was to know how often Evie would return to their family.

Although there were around a hundred and eighty institutions in Victoria at the time, it was a statistic that wasn't available to Leighton or the Lloyd family. Everyone was left to hope for the best, but Leighton wanted more than that for his sister.

Joey would say over and over again. 'An institution …'

If shouting could be soft, that was Arthur's voice. 'She is going. It's final, Joey.'

'Why can't we wait until she's older? She's so tiny; we're taking good care of her here. We can manage, Arthur.'

'Joey, you must understand. Evelyn has to be placed where she can learn a language, where she can get some sort of education. That can only happen outside the family. The doctor has told you that. The sooner it happens, the better for Evelyn.'

'How do we explain this to her?'

'We can't. She's a strong little girl and she will forgive us – forgive me – one day for sending her away. Even if you never do, Joey.'

'She'll be so afraid, away from all of us.'

'Joey, I know that. We all know that, but it's the sacrifice we must make if Evelyn is to have any hope of a future.'

'Arthur, how will we tell them all?'

'We'll do it together at teatime tomorrow.'

***

With chores completed and dinner eaten, the telling could not wait a moment longer. Arthur sat at the head of the table, with Evelyn on his knee where she could see everyone. Joey was outside, unable to bear witness to what was coming.

When Arthur spoke, everyone lowered their heads.

'Children, the doctor has told Mother that Evelyn is deaf and dumb.'

Leighton slipped down in his chair. A large bomb had been dropped inside the orange-warm kitchen. Left behind was the shrapnel of a family in shock.

Adeline was having none of it. 'What do you mean, Father?'

'Evelyn is deaf and dumb, and that means she will have to go to an institution.'

'But we can look after her here, she's never any trouble!'

'Yes, we can, but only for now. When she's six, she will go to Melbourne.'

Joey walked back into the room. 'Children, that's two years away,' she said. 'Until then, we will manage, and we won't talk about it anymore.'

Evelyn watched her people. Cliff stared through the table. Gwen folded her arms tighter across her chest. Leighton looked like he had fallen from a tree and been winded. Adeline looked ready for a fight, though this one she could never win.

'When the new baby comes, Evelyn will move in with the big girls,' Arthur said, changing the subject.

'A new baby? Since when?' Adeline asked.

'Since now.'

Gwen was already thinking. 'A new baby? What if—?'

'That's enough, children.' Joey wanted everything to stop. There was nothing left to say.

The family finally had a name for Evelyn's difference. Their all-things-bright-and-beautiful child was 'deaf and dumb'. And she would be at home for only two more years.

They were a family of good Christian soldiers and life had to keep moving forward. No-one would discuss how those two years would never be enough time to come to terms with the inevitable.

On 30 March 1923, Evelyn would turn six years old. The legal school age was what Joey had been dreading. An amendment to the *Education Act 1910* made the education of the 'deaf and dumb' compulsory. Family separation was preordained, and the Lloyd family would never break the law, not even for Evelyn.

Joey was too preoccupied to worry about other people's opinions. She let her mother tell the rest of the family. The news would spread fast in their small community.

14. GATHERING COURAGE

The future consisted of so many unknown circumstances. The older children continued to do what they had always done: Cliff skived off when he could, Leighton did his share of chores and spent every spare moment with Evelyn, and womanhood arrived early for Gwen and Adeline as they became responsible for even more adult chores. Everybody still pampered Evelyn, apart from her mother; Joey was preparing herself and Evelyn for what was to come.

Daily routines, family gatherings and church on Sundays took over. Added to these were visits to town to see the doctor, and to official bodies for signatures on paperwork that would finalise Evelyn's future. No-one had time to visit Melbourne for further information about the world of Deaf education.

Meanwhile, Evelyn would sneak into the dining room with the polished furniture and family treasures. There were angelic baby portraits of both Cliff and Gwen, but Leighton and Adeline had missed out. High up on the wall were large individual portraits of her and Father. He was elegant and thoughtful in his best suit, while at four years old she looked serious, innocent and pretty in her all-white outfit, with her ringlets and wide-eyed stare.

Keepsakes were few and precious, but there was something of Arthur left behind for posterity: the sword that he had carried back from the Boer War, that was always kept under the bed. Evelyn never saw it and Gwen never mentioned it, but somehow Adeline inherited it. Eventually, it found its way into the Wangaratta RSL.

***

Soon, a new distraction arrived – Evan Westall Lloyd, a gentle baby boy who responded to sounds and merged with the household. Now the sensory difference was clearer to Joey. From birth, Evelyn had that watchful way, alert and ready to make sense of the world.

Despite the birth of his new child, Arthur would still pick Evelyn up all the time.

'Arthur, she needs to become more independent.'

'You deal with Evelyn in your own way, Joey, and I'll deal with her in mine.

'Don't forget baby Evan,' replied Joey.

'Of course not, but he will always have his family close by,' said Arthur.

'So will Evelyn.'

'But never in the same way as our other children.'

'Evelyn will have to toughen up.'

'Promise me, Joey, that you won't let anyone hurt her.'

'Good God, Arthur, what do you think I am?'

***

Life kept nudging forward. Forgotten by everyone was how Evelyn was living on borrowed time. Two years passed quickly, and the day came for Joey and Arthur to once more talk about the future with their children.

'Children, we need to remind you …' Joey could not finish the sentence.

Arthur took over. 'Remember that Evelyn's going away soon, to school in Melbourne.'

Adeline pulled her shoulders back, as though she was speaking for them all. 'She's not even six! She doesn't have to go to school.'

'She will be six in two weeks, little miss,' said Joey.

'Evelyn will be educated in sign language,' Arthur added, trying to be gentle with his children. 'We hope she'll also learn to read and write.'

The other children knew better than to speak back to either of their parents, but Adeline would stand up for anyone, especially her little sister.

'But we know what she wants. And she's too little to go away.'

Suddenly, the weather outside took control and the sky opened up with a furious shower that diverted the entire household. Inside the house, a series of storms was also brewing. Everyone felt responsible for not doing enough to protect Evelyn; they all needed a way forward.

'She is leaving a week after her birthday,' Joey said.

'What sort of birthday present is that?' Adeline asked, marching off.

Leighton found his voice. 'Mother, why does Evie have to go away just yet?'

'She has to go to school, son.'

'It's too early. I can teach her; she's clever, she'll learn quickly. Mother, I promise you I will; I have already found ways. She'll be so frightened away from us, you know that.'

'I know, dear boy, but it's impossible. Time is up and we must let her go.'

The inevitable caught up with the family. Joey thought of Psalms 37:21: 'The wicked borrows but does not pay back, but the righteous is generous and gives.' Joey gave and gave, but nothing she had to give was ever enough.

Leighton understood that there was another world waiting for Evie, where she could meet people who were just like her. He had accepted his father's decision, but his heart breathed to the pulse of his mother's pain.

'Who will take her to Melbourne?' Gwen asked.

'That will be my job,' Arthur answered, reassuring her and himself. 'I'll be taking her in the buggy. I want to spend as much time with her as possible before she goes to school.'

Blame was one way to make sense of fate. If God was not to blame, then Joey blamed herself. Everything for Joey seemed to be a compromise: a Deaf education would have to be a trinity of hope, courage and sacrifice. Evelyn was being taken away to find her language in another world of belonging, and family acceptance would always be mixed with guilt, fear, shame, regret and never-ending love.

15. BIRTHDAY BLESSINGS

Before the future landed on their Bobinawarrah doorstep, there were things to be done in Oxley Shire. Life-changing decisions were like ghostly dancers whirling around the farmhouse. Evelyn was oblivious, but whenever she was dressed in her Sunday best it could also mean a visit to town. She liked those trips, especially for fabrics and clothes. The biggest store was perched on the corner of Murphy and Reid streets, decked out in an elegant outfit of Victorian architecture. The building was known as London House and it was home to the town's general drapery (in 1928 it would become known as WM Osmotherly's), as well as the place where people caught up with each other outside of church.

London House was built in 1860, just before the Lloyd and Wellington families arrived in the area. The grand façade of the majestic red-brick building featured brass-framed windows, with diamond-shaped stained-glass transoms and shiny moss-green tiles. Inside the double doors, an assortment of tactile images and diverse perfumes waited to be discovered. There were glass counters, wooden floors, mirrored walls and dressing rooms hidden by dark green velvet curtains that also served as bold backdrops for the clothes, shoes, fabrics, threads, ribbons and, her favourites, the jars of buttons in all colours, textures, shapes and sizes. Evelyn had learned early that clothes spoke their own language for Wellington women, and how the concept of 'waste not, want not' encouraged creativity.

For her upcoming birthday, and in preparation for her departure, aunties Phillipa, Ethel and even May had sewn for Evelyn three new school dresses, a best dress, two aprons, two nightdresses and undergarments. Auntie Ethel had also knitted a pair of warm gloves in the finest wool. There had been weekly trips into town for fabrics and trims, new boots, socks, hair ribbons and a soft coat made from local wool. Joseph Wellington had paid for everything on his account; it was the one thing he could do to pave the way for Evelyn and ease the pain for Joey.

Evelyn was everyone's favourite. She belonged to them all. But there was a sense of relief that it was Joey's daughter and not one of their own children who would have to go away.

Bobinawarrah birthdays took place at home, the church hall or the family homesteads of Tarramia or Waterloo. Summertime birthdays were often celebrated at the river. Busy lives often meant small, quick celebrations, with a new item of clothing as a gift and a slice of birthday cake. A child would have to wait until they turned twenty-one for a party and to receive a piece of heirloom jewellery. If you were married before then, well, your twenty-first was just another day for you.

For Evelyn, presents were not reserved for birthdays. She was often given gifts by people as a form of communication.

Her sixth birthday would be something to remember.

On that birthday night, the Wellington aunts appeared as soft shadows inside the mellow light of early evening. One by one, they carried forth food and presents. Over the past weeks, they had all been busy working on the small wardrobe they intended to give their cherished niece. Sisterhood was each meticulous stitch sewn with the gentlest care.

The last to arrive was Auntie Phillipa, with her three sons, including Vaughan. No-one had ever seen this other version of Vaughan, so subdued. Evelyn's leaving was significant for everybody in this close-knit family and community.

Centre stage was a cream sponge and the surprise was the cake's topping – a dome of home-grown strawberries sitting aloft a mountain of homemade whipped cream. Auntie Phillipa always did have an artist's touch.

'Dear girl, look … pretty cake.'

Evelyn smiled, pointed to herself.

'Yes, you.'

'Did you see that?' Arthur asked, impressed by his daughter's awareness.

Birthdays were a big day when you turned six. Evelyn's grandfather and her mother had taken her to town to buy new boots. She was wearing them for her birthday, and pointed to her feet to show Auntie Phillipa.

'Oh, they are very pretty! Just like you, little one.'

Evelyn's boots were made of soft black leather and had shiny buttons, ready for stepping into her new world. Auntie Phillipa bent over to touch the dainty boots. 'Now off you go, Evelyn. Let your busy feet take you to play with the other children.'

When the birthday girl left the room, Phillipa turned to her sister. 'Joey, it's such a heartache for you.'

'I don't know which way is up, Philly.'

'Remember how we felt when our brother was taken to the Royal Victorian Institute for the Blind?'

Joey had never forgotten that day. 'I hated it. And whenever we sent Charlie back there after the Christmas holidays, betrayal was what I always felt.'

'We all did, Joey.'

'This is different, though. He could tell us what he wanted or what he was feeling.'

'Joey, you'll find a place of acceptance. We all pray for that.'

'I doubt it, Philly – I very much doubt it.'

'Look at her, happily playing with Leighton and the other children.'

'That's another thing – how is that boy going to manage without her? How will any of us?'

'That's enough, now. We are going to enjoy Evelyn's party and that will cheer us all up, at least for now.'

Phillipa always knew when Joey and self-pity needed a hasty diversion. She didn't want Evelyn's special night to be ruined by what could never be fixed: her sister's broken heart.

16. NO TURNING BACK

'I am your God; I will strengthen you, I will help you, I will uphold you with my righteous right hand.' (Isaiah 41:10)

Right or left, neither hand could be the righteous or the redeemer for Joey. Sunday's church service held just another of God's unhelpful messages for the week ahead. Arthur's words circled in her mind: 'Evelyn's going away to the institution and that's final.' And Joey's last skerrick of courage was tested.

Conscience, commitment and contribution were the voices of women in the 1920s, but compromise contained neither faith nor hope. Joey had run out of time to explain her feelings to anyone, especially to Arthur. It sometimes seemed that he loved Evelyn more than he loved her, even though she was his wife.

In their bedroom, when Arthur touched her arm, Joey shook him off. She would find her own path forward, whatever that would take. And the way she would do that was not included in her marriage vows.

The final evening was imminent and Joey's shoulders had settled into a permanent shrug of despair. Her frantic thoughts raced to cures, home education, protection, too young, too small, too precious and even the possibility of an incorrect diagnosis. But she knew nothing would sway Arthur.

'The quicker Joey accepts that Evelyn has a future in Melbourne, the better for everyone,' Arthur had said to his eldest brother Charlie.

'I wouldn't want to be in your shoes,' Charlie had replied, relieved that this was not happening to his own family.

The day was approaching, but there would be no second coming to resurrect this family. Arthur would not let their unbearable sacrifice overwhelm the personal commitment he had made to himself, Joey and their daughter.

People asked each other why Arthur was taking Evelyn all the way to Melbourne in the horse and buggy. It was a three-day journey, long for anyone but especially so for a small child. Arthur tried to explain himself to his brother.

'Charlie, I know what people are saying, but there are too many distractions on the train. I need to spend as much time with her as possible. Who knows what will happen this year.'

'Brother, it will be you picking her up at Christmas time, God willing.'

'I hope you're right. And let's hope I don't break any more promises.'

***

As preparations were taking place, distant storm clouds gathered. A cleansing rain might benefit the crops, but no amount of rain could ever wash away the sadness of this last night.

'Arthur, let her sit with the other children.' Joey said.

His knee was always where Evelyn sat. 'She likes it here, where she can see everyone.'

'There'll be no knees to sit on in that place.'

Evelyn watched voice shapes and thought, *Mother cross – me.* Her fault, and maybe also her father's. 'Cross' and 'sad' were separate expressions, but it was beyond anyone to understand what to say or do on their final evening together.

'Evelyn's eaten her dinner, she can get down now. Eat your own, Arthur. You have a long journey ahead.'

Later, when they were alone, Arthur chided his wife, saying, 'Joey, you know I have Evelyn with me at the table to make her feel safe.'

'Safe? God knows what's going to happen to her soon. She won't be able to tell us if something's wrong.'

'Joey, it's best for everyone.'

'It's me who'll pick up the pieces you'll leave behind, Arthur.' Joey had started and could not stop. 'There's too much to be done, and I won't be able to go to Melbourne at the drop of a hat.'

'It won't come to that. You're tired—'

'Tired! That's the least of it. Arthur, I just don't know where to begin, or where all this will end … Can't anyone see that I'm her mother?'

'She's a special child. She needs to go away to learn.' He was ready for the process, but not for the hurt caused.

'Don't you dare to tell me about how precious it is to be different! This is too hard for everyone, especially for her.'

'There's nothing that's too hard to manage.'

'That's not true. You don't understand why I'm upset,

Arthur. No-one could possibly understand.' Joey could no longer contain her hurt. 'What will we do without her?' Joey kept going. Anger was all she had left. 'How will she feel when you leave her there, Arthur? Have you thought of that?'

'Someone has to follow this decision through, and that someone is me.'

Joey felt unable to protect her child. In her own eyes and heart, she felt she had failed all her children, especially her dearest little girl, so young she still sucked her thumb.

17. PREPARATION – SEPARATION

For six years Evelyn and her difference had kept the family united, but navigating this change would use up any resilience they had left. Arthur and Evelyn were set to begin their journey towards another language and cultural world.

Country life had not yet heard of miracles like Helen Adams Keller, born in 1880, just three years before Joey. Helen was the first deaf and blind person to achieve a university degree. However, distance was not only measured in miles, it covered attitudes and ideas as well. America was many worlds away, a place where sign language and new ideas about deafness were taking place, light years ahead of Australia. Many people were developing a sense of identity in the Deaf world, but that world was foreign to the Lloyd and Wellington families.

Inclusivity was not a word people used at that time. Solutions meant separation, even for a much-loved four-senses child who could skilfully skim-read her farm world. Crossing over to another world of language and culture would allow Evelyn to fill the empty spaces of what could not be explained to her.

She knew nothing about Deaf history or deafness as a

primary sense for understanding the world, or about what was missing and what could never be. Broken by what she could not solve or control, there was one important thing that could have put Joey's mind at ease, if she'd known at that time. Over ninety percent of deaf children are born to hearing parents.

In Oxley Shire at that time, there was no-one else quite like Evelyn. Of course, there were other children in other country towns who were classified as 'deaf and dumb', and their parents also had to make heartbreaking decisions. However, farm life meant it was difficult for Joey to meet other parents in similar situations to her.

Everyone was overwhelmed, including Arthur, but he knew that the Victorian Deaf and Dumb Institution in Melbourne was Evelyn's only chance in life. She would meet other children like her who came from all over the state, and from other parts of Australia, to attend the school. Any other choice would compromise her intellect and Arthur would never allow that, not while he still had breath in his body.

There had already been too many hushed nights when not even the softness of lamplight could make cyclical thoughts and conversations about Evelyn and her future any clearer. Arthur and Joey had prayed out loud and to themselves, but there was not enough faith or language to explain the future, especially to Evelyn.

'Institution – what a word. Call it "school", that'll make it easier, Joey,' said Arthur, also struggling with this decision.

'School, institution, whatever you want to call it, it's in Melbourne, not down the jolly road,' Joey retaliated.

'I haven't even seen where Evelyn is going,' said Adeline.

'Father will see it soon and tell you all about it.'

'Have you visited the school, Mother?' Gwen asked.

'We went past it on the tram when we were in Melbourne.'

'Why didn't you go inside?'

'I can barely remember what happened that day, there was so much going on.'

'But we need to know what that place is like!' insisted Adeline.

'It might be best if we don't.'

'Evelyn will be with other children like her,' said Arthur, attempting a voice of reason.

'I'm her sister! No-one can be any more like her than her own sister!'

'Stop it, Adeline.' Gwen knew there would never be one answer that could satisfy everyone. Cliff and Leighton were outside completing chores, and just this once she wished she could join them.

The arrangements for Evelyn's schooling had been made over a number of months with the local doctor and Justice of the Peace in Wangaratta. Official decisions held a voice of authority that was difficult to explain to the children. Many official discussions and phone calls had taken place, the men in charge of it all. Any visit for Joey or Arthur to Melbourne over the last two years had been impossible since there was so much to be considered in order to make the trip – the five other children, finances, Arthur's illness, the farm to manage and the risk of upsetting Evelyn. So, father and daughter would see the school at the same time. Whether that was a good idea or not was never discussed.

'Mother, it's so awful to think—'

'Enough, Gwen. Enough!' Silenced by her father, Gwen could not begin to imagine her little Lambie in that foreign place. Neither could anyone else.

'No more for today, children. There's too much to be done.' The last say from Joey didn't mean much.

Tomorrow was on its way, rain, hail or shine. Joey wanted some control over her child's comforts, even if it was only providing blankets, clothes and food. She went over everything that would be needed again and again. But she could not pack what Evelyn would need most: her family.

18. HOME COMFORTS

Early on, Gwen had noticed that baby Evelyn could always be soothed by touching fabric. Auntie Phillipa helped with sewing lessons and taught Gwen how to stitch and stuff a small rag doll for her little sister. There were even tiny stitches for the facial features. Evelyn carried that doll everywhere.

Blankets were the voice of soft, warm comfort that held everyone inside their home place, especially Evelyn. There was one blanket, cream-coloured and made from fluffy wool, that Evelyn liked to hold when she was placed into her bed at night. The day before departure there had been a breezy sunshine, the perfect time to wash the small cot blanket. The whole family knew it was her blanket of belonging; Joey had even taken it with them when they took the train to Melbourne.

On the last night, everyone was disturbed. After a dessert of apple pie and cream, Evelyn's favourite, she was bathed and dressed in her old nightgown. It was a bit small, so it hadn't been packed in her suitcase. Then, without any warning, the hushed house erupted. Evelyn was crying, wheezing, stamping her feet; her troubled tears made everyone want to let go and cry along with her.

'What's wrong with Evelyn?' Cliff asked.

'She's upset about something,' Adeline said.

'I can see that, Miss Know-It-All, but what does she want?'

No-one could work out what was wrong with Evelyn. Her distress was too frightening to identify.

'Do you think she knows she's being taken away?' he asked.

'She knows something's going on,' Adeline replied.

'But she gets everything she wants.'

'Cliff, how would you like it?'

'What? Going away?'

'Stupid boy ...' But Adeline was unable to explain to anyone, let alone herself.

Adeline found Evelyn's rag doll and the basket of fabrics.

'Here you go, Evelyn.'

The basket and doll were shoved aside. Evelyn's upset was rare. The crying, wheezing and foot stamping were not the testing part for Joey. The last straw was something else.

'My God, what if this happens when she's at school? I can't bear to think of it.'

'Mother, don't take the Lord's name in vain,' Gwen muttered.

'It's alright, Mother,' said Adeline. 'We just need to think this through.'

Leighton could usually guess what she wanted, but not this time. He had gone outside to pat the dog. There was only so much he could take and he was unable to watch the night fall apart for a moment longer. They all wanted to do what Leighton had done – wrap their arms around themselves and escape. Brave children that they were, they would wait until they were alone to indulge their own hurt.

'Hurry up, someone find out what she wants,' said Cliff, his heart breaking.

'Let's start at the beginning,' suggested Gwen. 'What happened this morning when Evelyn got out of bed?'

'The same thing as every other day.'

'Cliff, there's nothing the same about this day or this night.' Gwen said through her teeth.

By then, Joey was desperate. 'I went into her room to get her blanket, to wash it for the trip.'

'Where's the blanket now?'

'Good God! It's still outside on the line! I wanted the breeze to soften it for her.'

'I'll get it. We'll see if that's the problem.' Gwen ran outside.

'Can't I get anything right?' Joey asked, as the question fell flat at her feet.

The cloud-filled night sky was bruised black and blue. Wide open to the elements, Evelyn's blanket flapped and floated across the slow undercurrent of a Bobinawarrah breeze. At the rough clothesline, Gwen pulled down the two old wooden pegs, gathered the softness of the blanket to her face and rubbed it against her jaw. She inhaled wool and night air and prepared to march back inside, but not until she wiped her wet eyes on the sleeve of her cardigan.

'Lambie, look what I found!' Gwen's secret name for Evelyn was now out in the open.

Evelyn ran to her big sister; Gwen always knew how to

fix things. The blanket was back where it belonged and the tone in the room shifted and settled. With peace in the kitchen, the family saviour was nearly forgotten in the fuss.

'Thank goodness you realised the blanket was missing.' Arthur had escaped the noise and frustration by hooking up the horse and buggy. He had not gone to the pub; instead he spent time under the infinite night sky collecting his resolve. 'Good girl, Gwennie. What would we ever do without you?'

'Thank you, Father.' On this peculiar evening, Gwen found it easier to forgive him for her disappointments.

There was one habit that was never discussed. The way Evelyn would wrap her blanket around her hand, hold it close to her face and suck her thumb before she fell asleep. She kept a tight hold on the blanket every night and sometimes even throughout the day. Joey had said a silent prayer that her daughter would grow out of this stage before she had to go away, but she soon realised it was too much to expect a child to compromise her language of comfort.

Bedtime arrived and Joey wanted to warn the children, but more so herself.

'Tomorrow, you must not let Evelyn see you upset. We can't explain, so be brave for her.'

'Mother, this is awful. We must find a way to tell her what's happening.'

'Adeline, if we could, we would.'

'Leave Mother alone, Adeline,' said Leighton.

'Mind your own business.' But the battle was fading for the little girl warrior. 'I'm going to bed.'

Inside their small room, Gwen and Adeline were still the two big sisters who shared a bed and chores, but their secrets and their hurts they mostly kept to themselves.

Evelyn's four senses jumped this way and that. She absorbed household smells and the leftover taste of apple pie and cream. Soothed by her found blanket, she sucked her thumb and picked at the peeling paint on her cot.

Earlier that day, Adeline had stood watching Evelyn from the bedroom door. Her tiny head had tilted to the left as she traced her hands in quizzical curiosity across the worn leather suitcase. The suitcase, the Melbourne trip, Mother never quite the same. The change was not visual, but more a presence that had come to stay.

Determined not to let anyone see her cry, fortitude straightened Adeline's shoulders. 'Tears are for sooky bubs!' she shouted into the kitchen.

When they were in bed together, Gwen wrapped her arms around her sister. Everyone had forgotten that Adeline was only nine years old. Wanting Evelyn to stay in this room with them forever, they shared the same silent wish that tomorrow would never come.

Gwen stayed awake, listening to the bedroom breathing. At thirteen, she was not Evelyn's mother, nor Adeline's, but she felt a mother's sadness.

Outside the house, the chill of the crisp evening stunned Joey. The shadowy fig tree was bursting with budding fruit. Evelyn loved playing under this tree, eating the figs, putting the jam on fresh bread. That night, Joey let her thoughts meander from one thing to another.

She thought about last Sunday's church service. 'Keep

your heart with all vigilance, for from it flow the springs of life.' (Proverbs 4:23) Joey Lloyd had been a vigilant mother, but it seemed to her as if it had not been enough.

Through the gaps of evening and beyond into the distance, the purple-shadowed mountains stood silent and sad. Joey pictured her sister Emmeline and remembered the time when they had shared a bed, their dreams and their secrets. Her faraway sister was the one person that Joey could trust with her fears and who could comfort her. Simple words like, 'Joey, this too shall pass.'

Once again, life found its own way forward. Courage willed her forth, but for now, hope was well-hidden behind Mount Misery. There would be no-one turning up to make this night any easier. But alone that night, it came to Joey that she was the one who had heard the gentle sound of Evelyn taking her first breath.

19. FAREWELLS

Wednesday was the day of the leaving. The trip ahead would take three full days. Sunday clothes had been set out on the dining room table, ready and waiting. The leather seats of the buggy were well sprung and the cart had a bleached canvas cover for rain or cooler weather. On the tray of the buggy, Joey had placed the suitcase, bags, blankets, clothes and food, all covered with a thick layer of home. She had thought of everything, even what did not bear thinking about.

It surprised her that she knew how to move. Her hands – large, flat, worn and hardworking – placed the cream-coloured wool soother into her daughter's tiny hands. Early April meant cold mornings and sunny days; both father and child would need to stay warm. She tucked one of the thick, warm, woollen blankets from the house around Evelyn, preparing her for the journey. But there was nothing on this earth or beyond that could ever prepare Joey for letting go.

Sibling eyes looked away. They had all noticed how Evelyn's tiny black leather boots did not reach the floor of the buggy. Evelyn was proud of her birthday gift, although the brown boots in the store were her preference; Joey had watched her touching them. The school list had indicated that all footwear must be black.

'Who will do up Evelyn's shoes?'

'Be quiet, Adeline.' Cliff often did that small task for Evelyn.

Against the dusky sky, the lilac tree stooped beneath a veil of deep purple tears. Safe hands held the horse's reins as her father looked ahead, and the patient horse was ready.

In that last moment, familiar arms held her a bit too tight. Then Joey held her child's face gently, and kissed her dainty daughter on the forehead. The time had come; Joey's hands opened wide and she let go and surrendered Evelyn to her future.

In her darkest hour, she took her longest walk back towards her other children, then turned to stand with them, all bunched together. Hands were raised in unison as they wiped away tears and waved farewell to Evelyn. Making something from nothing would require a bit more effort on everyone's part that day.

The horse pulled forward and Evelyn fell back deeper into her seat. Beneath the Bobinawarrah sky everything was still familiar and she thought she would be back home soon after a short adventure with Father.

She could see the roads ahead – church road, town road, picnic road, river road and roads leading to grandparents, aunts, uncles and cousins. The brown leather case and new boots suggested a journey, not a visit, but she didn't know where they were going. She trusted her father to know everything, but this was not the road they took to the river, to church or to town. This trip must be important, as he was wearing his Sunday-best suit, and a badge in his lapel that signified his RSL membership, recognition of his service in the Boer War. He was a local legend, but to Evelyn her father was God and her hero.

This trip to Melbourne required a different kind of courage from that of the much younger man who had left home and country to conquer all he did not know about the world. The long three-day journey ahead would allow Arthur time to contemplate his precious daughter's future and reflect upon his own life.

20. UNKNOWN FUTURES

My grandfather's experiences were not unusual – they were chapters characteristic of the wider Australian experience of the time. His life may be seen as ordinary until the day he took his little daughter on a three-day journey down Sydney Road.

Arthur and Evelyn are the only two people who know the story of their long-ago trip to Melbourne, but everyone knows stories have a life of their own. As their direct descendant, I have given myself permission to interpret what may have happened during that time in my own way.

***

Arthur had not shared his plans for that first day. It was only he who knew they would travel from Bobinawarrah to Euroa, a total of sixty-three miles (just over one hundred kilometres), and that their journey would be done in separate stages. Their early start began before sunrise on 3 April 1923.

As they set out, left behind was their household of early risers, and swallowed up by the early morning light was the road back to Evelyn's world. Daylight waited where the crossroads met at Winton and readied to join Sydney Road.

That road would take Arthur and Evelyn to Benalla, Violet Town and a long way beyond.

Evelyn, seated high in the buggy, watched as the countryside merged images of place. Arthur wanted this time with his daughter to explain some of his history to her, how important she was to him and what would be waiting for her at the end of their journey together.

The chestnut-coloured horse was steady and sure-footed. He kept trotting along, ever ready to change direction if needed. When he led them through Greta West, Arthur tried to capture history for Evelyn.

'This is near where the bushranger Ned Kelly and his family lived. What a ratbag! There's nothing like a Ned Kelly story, and everyone has more than one. Evelyn, you don't have to do much in Australia to be famous. Rob the Euroa National Bank like the Kelly Gang, get two thousand pounds and become an Australian hero.'

The horse kept trotting and Arthur continued: 'I was only three years old in eighteen seventy-eight, when it happened. People still talk about the gang to this very day. I'll be forgotten when I go, but no-one will ever forget that bloody Ned Kelly. Or you, Evelyn, my darling girl.'

Under Arthur's guidance, the horse established a steady tempo. The pace allowed Arthur to tell Evelyn what he knew about the world.

'Ned's tough old mum had a sly grog shop here. She was a widow with young kids, so I guess she had to earn her living somehow. Those old slab walls must've heard a thing or two.'

Silent scenery stretched out into a wider world of ghostly gum trees, wooden bridges, crystal-clear winding creeks, brown rolling rivers, animals running through the bush, and towering, rock-cropped mountains that came from nowhere.

Arthur tapped Evelyn's arm and pointed. 'Look, Evelyn, kangaroos watching, see them in the bush? Cheeky beggars.'

Her blue-grey stare soon found a new rhythm as it moved between her father's face and the unknown road ahead.

'Evelyn, you're going to school. Everyone needs a language. I'm sad to say that yours can only be found far away from the farm and from us.'

Overwhelmed by the strength of his actions and surprised by the sound of his own thoughts, he wanted to explain what was happening to Evelyn, but more so to himself.

'Everybody has moments when courage goes missing and dreams, faith and hope are fragile. When we're alone, it can be hard to keep going, but we always do. And you, little one, always will.'

Arthur believed in this child. He had to look forward, or he would turn around and take her straight back home. Evelyn looked at him as if she could understand his every word. He patted the blanket covering her leg. Arthur felt heard by her, but too many things would be left unsaid.

'I'll keep to myself what happened in the war, Evelyn. My mother – the grandmother you never met – was the only person with whom I could share those memories. I wasn't a hero; I did what must be done. And that's what I'm doing with our journey.

'We all need to share our stories with someone. You do that with Leighton, don't you? I do hope he can learn your language one day. I don't think the others will have the inclination.'

Arthur wondered if he too would have the ability to learn the language of sign for Evelyn's sake. Taking time to learn another language would be near impossible, but crossing certain bridges could only be done when he came to them.

'Everyone loves you, child, but I know they're also glad it's not them who can't hear the birds, music or farm sounds. Or the wonderful joy of Mother's singing.' Arthur knew his comments were disloyal, but his deepest truths travelled with them along Sydney Road.

'Don't forget that your family and home will always be there for you.'

Arthur usually saw himself as an ordinary man, but now he had a chance to make a difference. Aside from the way his mother had loved and cared for him, he had never been loved so simply as he had been loved by Evelyn. He trusted that his mother and daughter seemed to understand his intentions and see past his faults.

There would be some responsibilities he would never complete. Arthur had tried – his last will and testament was set in place and he was fortunate to have a wife and daughters who were as capable as any man. But there was only so much that he could do now. He could guide Evelyn and the horse, but her future was beyond even his prayers.

As they travelled along the road through a soft shower of rain, the light changed and the countryside was painted in brighter shades of greys, greens and browns. Gum trees lined the way, and they passed country towns that supported farming families and goldmining hopefuls. They drove past rough bush, rivers, creeks and bridges. Evelyn could see how the simple cottages, grander houses, banks and town halls either imposed on or crept up into the landscape. The hills and trees pushed forward and faded away as Sydney Road slowly advanced towards Melbourne.

Reflection time for Arthur went beyond his experiences of the war. There were the fun trips he had taken as a young man to Mount Buffalo, when he had been more like his son Cliff than he cared to admit. His thoughts also turned to money. The yearly institution fees were two pounds and seven shillings; they had to be found. His family's unspoken grief was the real cost. But nothing could shake away his foremost thought: taking her there and, more importantly, collecting her back home.

All day, they watched a passing parade of men and women dressed in their Sunday best, driving horses and buggies. Some were even driving cars, like Grandfather Wellington. Unknown futures for people of every ilk; they travelled the same road, but for different reasons. Men on horseback waved and Arthur waved back. Evelyn lifted her hand, snug and warm inside Auntie Ethel's hand-knitted glove, and waved too. She was a social child, something that had always delighted Arthur.

'Clever girl, saying hello.'

Soon they could see Euroa, the wool-producing town nestled in the foothills of the Strathbogie Ranges.

It was nightfall when they finally arrived. Their first day's journey had been around twelve hours of travel time.

Along the way, Arthur had stopped to stretch his legs

and for Evelyn to refresh herself. They ate Joey's wholesome food, and there were still apples and fruitcake left over for the following day. Despite the fresh air and country scenes, it had been a long journey. One world was behind them and another world waited ahead.

'Euroa is where we are stopping for the night, Evelyn. I've heard that the name means "joyful" in the local Aboriginal language. There are so many languages in the world, and you'll find yours one day – sooner rather than later, I hope.'

Tired, Evelyn stroked her blanket and sucked her thumb as she thought of the evening routine taking place at home.

The large country town of Euroa was a popular stopover destination and had a range of accommodation choices for travellers. Seven Creeks Hotel was the oldest and most frequented hotel in Euroa, and was Arthur and Evelyn's place of rest for that night.

Grandfather Wellington had made sure that money for this trip was not an extra concern. Arthur had accepted the family charity; his pride might be compromised but never Evelyn's comfort. A restful night was required as tomorrow would be another long day.

Arthur took Evelyn with him to the stone stables, where he unhitched the buggy and tended to the horse, a familiar routine in an unfamiliar place. Beer and companionship were what he needed, but that night he drank outside. A glass of raspberry lemonade delighted Evelyn as the bubbles tickled her nose, another surprise on their adventure. Joey would never know that her child had been so near to a pub; Arthur would never tell and neither would Evelyn.

***

The next stage of the trip would take them from Euroa to Kilmore. It was once again around sixty miles (nearly one hundred kilometres). Arthur was interested to see how the countryside would change the closer they got to Melbourne. They would travel via Seymour, Tallarook and Broadford. Another twelve to thirteen hours in the buggy, but the rested horse was ready and willing to repeat the rhythms of the day before, content to move his charges forward.

Stories, memories and history flowed together; Bobinawarrah folklore was a river that flowed through cultures and generations.

Arthur said, 'Evelyn, one day you will know how your descendants settled the area where we live. The "Farmers Five", they were called.'

A first-generation Australian, Arthur was proud of his pioneering father and uncle and thought they had chosen their land well. He wanted Evelyn to be included in her family history. Home was the family farm and he thought it always would be that way, with sons to take over from him.

Father and daughter continued on. When they crossed a fast-flowing waterway, another story came to Arthur's mind.

'Evelyn, one day you might wonder how Bobinawarrah was given such a funny name, so let me tell you about Bob Montgomery and West Hurdle Creek.

'Belfast-born Robert Montgomery, one of the Farmers Five, had settled near the creek. He built his property there,

Glenview, not far from where my father built his. That's the homestead where your Auntie Phillipa, Uncle Charlie and your cousins live today.

'Now, eighteen eighty-six was a very wet year. At one point, all the rain caused the creek to flood. With his ginger hair and beard, Bob was well known by the locals. On the day of the flood, Bob went to the Gibb farm on horseback to check the cattle. There he found many stranded over on the other side of Hurdle Creek, and decided to bring them back to higher and safer ground. Cattle were as valuable as gold then. Still are.

'Bravely or foolishly, Bob entered the flooding creek and started moving the frightened animals, but he soon got into difficulty. A rushing river stops for no man, and poor old Bob was swept off his horse.

'A few people had gathered to watch, including some of the local Aboriginal people. Bob somehow got out of the river and lived to tell the tale. It was thought at the time that "warrah" meant "water" in the language of the locals. So Bobinawarrah was named for "Bob in a water".'

Arthur laughed, and so did Evelyn. Arthur, like all his children, would chuckle when he told or heard a good story. And one of his favourite things about Evelyn was how she could always see the funny side of things, even without hearing the full story.

Father and daughter sat in companionable silence. The road continued through rough and undulating country. But when they reached the tail end of the Great Dividing Range, the road climbed up nearly five hundred and fifty yards (over five hundred metres); not excessive, but enough to slow their advance.

The sky spread in all directions as the evening closed in on them. There was another hotel to organise, the horse to rest and a good night's sleep to be had in preparation for the final leg of the journey and another life for Evelyn.

***

On the third day, they travelled from Kilmore to Prahran, a shorter distance of forty-five miles (approximately seventy-five kilometres), and the last stage of their trip. Evelyn sensed their journey was ending; the horse was getting tired and her father could only concentrate on the road ahead.

There was a brief moment when Arthur considered that maybe train travel would have been easier for the child, but he quickly dismissed the thought.

They passed through Beveridge and Kalkallo, all the while keeping to Sydney Road. In Coburg, on the outskirts of Melbourne, they passed one of Australia's most famous jails, Pentridge Prison. Closer to the city, the road changed into a busy place and both Arthur and horse became absorbed in finding the way forward. Unlike Evelyn's open Bobinawarrah sky, buildings blocked out the heavens here.

Soon they were negotiating Melbourne's roads. Arthur was trying to find his way to St Kilda Road in Prahran, but it was difficult as he had not made this particular trip before. The height of the buildings imposed upon his sense of direction. Up until that moment, his senses had always been good, but now they were being tested, along with his resolve.

21. A NEW BEGINNING

Arthur had hoped the trek on that last day would be shorter, but it took over nine hours to reach Prahran. The traffic had slowed their progress and they arrived in the late afternoon. He had wanted Evelyn to see her school in the daylight. The neo-Gothic architecture of the school appeared before them. Church-like but not a church, the large, bleak building of the Victorian Deaf and Dumb Institution dominated the landscape.

In their three days of travelling, Evelyn had watched everything around her, slept well and never been a moment's trouble. Arthur had found many words for her and himself, and had even prayed to God. Staying on task, he had kept driving forward, although at times it was only the horse who was in charge.

Sacrifice was a load too heavy for this ordinary man. Choice was not a fair option; the opportunity for an education for Evelyn was all he had left, his most precious gift to her. Overshadowed by tall towers rising from the strange building were the fading images of the Bobinawarrah world they had left behind. Scrutinised by soaring walls of bluestone blocks and towering turrets was the man who believed his all-things-bright-and-beautiful child was wise and wonderful and deserved to learn. Together they could only stare at the steeple spikes that stabbed through an unfamiliar sky.

The double doors etched with biblical images beckoned the father and daughter inside. The doors were opened by a man wearing a city suit and an affable smile. After three full days of travel, Arthur was still wearing his church suit, although he had changed his shirt and polished his shoes before leaving Kilmore that morning. Joey had instructed him to dress Evelyn in clean clothes, and he had also done that. Presentation was everything in the Lloyd family.

Fear and Arthur had met many times. Neither one could win, but Arthur always had respect for the battle that took place. The return journey would leave time enough for him to ponder his doubts and remember what he wanted to forget.

Arthur observed Evelyn, with her soft sounds and gentle grace. Perhaps she was ready to make sense of the world – always watching, skim-reading people and waiting for what would happen next. Back home, Evelyn had never seemed this small. Now here she was, her tiny hands holding tight to the last touch and smells of her home – her cream blanket and her father.

'Everyone will love you, Evelyn, like we all do,' he said.

But the early evening smells of this place were unfamiliar. They were not those of the farm's kitchen, of the lilac and apple trees, or of Evelyn's people. Arthur saw that the memories of all that was missing were too much for Evelyn. She grew frightened; her expressive face told him so.

Guilt had travelled along the long road with Arthur.

He wondered if a woman's guilt was the same as that of a man. He was prepared to take any hits coming his way, had trained himself for this final challenge. He had promised himself that he would never leave his child in a place where she would be unsafe, yet on this particular piece of Prahran earth, thy will be done.

'Don't be afraid, little one. There will be children just like you here.'

Daylight disappeared, replaced by twilight shadows and the pungent smells of a distant teatime. The sandwiches, fruitcake and apples her mother had packed were now all gone. Her mother and her siblings would be eating dinner together in the family kitchen, and wondering what she and Father might be doing now.

It was difficult for her not to think of home, with its safe evening aromas of cooking, cow yards, the orchard and herbs at the back door. Now the sour smell of rising damp signalled displacement and separation. Doors opened and closed with new people, and everything she had ever known was well beyond this place. Familiar family hands and their gentle touches had gone missing.

At that time, difference belonged elsewhere. The bold architecture of the Institution was set well back from busy St Kilda Road, but the imposing building made its presence felt nonetheless. The location was central to trams and trains, and the city was close by. Evelyn, as a 'deaf and dumb' child, was defined as different in her family and the community. Her new environment would both confuse and redefine her conflicting sense of belonging.

Doubt and distrust spilled over into her world and she

struggled to make sense of her place inside each unexplained moment. How could she know that beyond the unfamiliar doors a new tribe was waiting for her to join them?

Sad mouth shapes were coming from her father.

'All children fear separation from their parents, my girl. I even felt that when I went to South Africa. I missed my family every day, as you will.'

Arthur was a man of few words, but on this trip he had not stopped talking and he did not seem to be able to finish everything he had to say to her.

'Everyone at home will be thinking about you, more often than you'll be thinking of them. You'll soon be busy making friends and finding your language.'

Evelyn watched as her father folded the blankets, slow and careful, to take back home. Arthur knew that back in Bobinawarrah, when no-one was watching, Joey would hold every soft fabric that Evelyn had touched close to her nose. And he knew that to keep the scent of her child with her, Joey would not wash those blankets for a very long time. He lifted the leather suitcase, heavy with the weight of home, from the buggy with the gentlest of care. He wanted to turn around and take her straight back home, but he knew he could not. Instead, he carried Evelyn and her suitcase through the double doors. She had one hand around his neck and the other holding her comfort blanket, and together they went towards her future.

As he recuperated at his sister Ethel's house that terrible night and the next day, the story that Arthur told himself was that he meant the last words he had said to his daughter: 'Darling girl, I will come back and get you. I promise.'

22. GIRL 735

Everything about that night was alien to Evelyn. Suddenly, a strange woman wearing a high-buttoned blouse and a long, heavy, brown skirt appeared. She stepped forward and touched Evelyn's shoulder. The woman held her hand as they headed up the grand staircase. When they paused on the landing before taking the next set of stairs, Evelyn saw something from her church world. The soaring colours of a large stained-glass window spoke to her of home. Three lofty panels showed an angel with a yellow light above her head and, on either side of her, two cherubs floating above biblical scrolls with unknown words.

> *'And in that day the deaf will hear words read from a book.*
> *He maketh both the deaf to hear, and the dumb to speak.'*

Apart from the picturesque window reminding her of sunlit Sundays, this world was dark and ominous as she tried to make sense of where the cavernous building started and finished. The smell of wet wool, stale food and unfamiliar bodies was distasteful to her. The journey with her father had been an adventure, but this was more like a bad dream.

There was nothing else she could do but hold tight to the hand of the strange woman who made unusual mouth and hand shapes. Trust had been foremost in Evelyn's life; now it was gone. Father had deserted her, and she sensed he would not be back anytime soon.

Another large door was opened and the woman took Evelyn into a room bigger than her own house. The woman unpacked Evelyn's brown leather suitcase and the hand-stitched contents were placed in Locker 735. She would come to know that number well.

Although she was still Evelyn, she would now officially be known as 'Girl 735'.

Strange building, strange smells, strange light inside a strange room that overflowed with strange girls of all shapes and sizes who were lined up against two rows of similar grey-blanketed beds that faced each other. Surprised by the animated faces and hands that were sitting, pointing, swiping, slapping and staring, Evelyn could only stare back, transfixed.

All eyes were on the woman. Her hands, fingers and face moved with a swiftness that Evelyn had never seen before. Everyone else seemed to follow this visual language: one hand across the back of the other hand for the word 'new', and an index finger moved across the cheek for 'girl.' Evelyn, without yet knowing, was the 'new girl.'

The girls and the teacher used their hands in the same way, and again she was the centre of attention. Nothing made sense, but comfort might be found with these girls through their moving hands and spirited faces.

The wooden floors of the school made unfamiliar

vibrations beneath her new boots. She barely knew how to dress or undress, so the woman helped her. Later, it would be one of the big girls until she could do it herself.

It was dark outside and inside. Evelyn was ready for sleep to take over, but not before her thoughts found their way back to her cosy bedroom on the farm. It was her safe space, where her bare feet could feel the contrast between the smooth linoleum floor and the pink rag rug. Every night before her two big sisters went to sleep in the double bed, they would tuck her into her cot and kiss her goodnight as her hands caressed the soft, washed quilt. Surely they would be missing her, because she was definitely missing them.

That night, her only comfort inside the unknown darkness was the touch of her soft blanket and her thumb.

***

When Girl 735 woke, she could see the same rows of beds and the same girls from the night before. In the daylight, things began falling into place.

The upstairs girls' dormitory was across the passage from the boys' dormitory, the bathrooms and a nurse's room. Downstairs were classrooms, the dining room and large outdoor spaces. Everywhere was an unbroken body of communication and connection.

Evelyn's first day was filled with children showing her around and playing games in the grounds. Every child had been a new boy or girl until they were given their locker number. That was how they were identified at first, until they found other ways to say their personal names – initials or abbreviations or a one-syllable word like E-V-E. Easy to spell in sign language, it quickly became her name in the Deaf world.

The next day, Evelyn sensed Sunday must be close. She had not been to church for many days; five days away from home with two nights in this place. Last Sunday, she had attended the Milawa church. On this morning, the bigger children did chores and the younger children played on the grounds. She liked being included in their play. Her new world was shifting in all directions, instant, constant and plausible.

Stillness was not part of this place. She witnessed something these children shared between themselves – everyone was a skim-reader and they could all follow each other. They were all comfortable jumping from one set of talking hands to another. Evelyn sensed it would not take her long to join them; her hands had always had a mind of their own.

Her heartache could not be forgotten, but she soon recognised that she was in the middle of an adventure with other children who could help her understand her place in the world.

Food defined the main difference between farm and school. While the roast lunch was simple and wholesome, it was tasteless to her. It had none of the robust flavours of home. Thoughts of shared meals carried her back to the farm, to roaming with Leighton, the bossy brown rooster, and the breakfasts of warm, nutty porridge topped with fresh honey and cream. School porridge was grey, watery milk.

Anytime she had a spare moment, she remembered her people gathered for her birthday. Spread across the carved dining table and best lace tablecloth was farm-fresh food, with Auntie Phillipa's cream sponge with strawberries piled high in the middle. Now that she was wearing her new clothes and boots, she could understand why she had been given so many gifts.

Endless adjustments were made to her new environment. At home, her people moved to a gentle, steady rhythm and created protective spaces for her. Inside this strange new world of thumping activity and dragging furniture, animated bodies took their places at the dining room table. Children slapped shoulders, stamped feet and banged tables to capture each other's attention. The boisterous boys bothered Evelyn – her Lloyd boys were sometimes cheeky and silly, but never unruly.

The place was bursting with individual personalities expressing themselves. Children who were erratic and withdrawn showed their anxieties in the only ways they knew how. Evelyn came to understand their ways, as she recalled her own rare tantrums to make herself understood. The majority of children were happy to be with others like themselves, discovering their language and culture. And Evelyn, with her quiet nature and delightful sense of humour, was soon as much loved in this new world as she was back at the farm.

23. PUTTING PIECES TOGETHER

Life at school found its own way forward, with five days of schooling in sign language and weekends of play that were sometimes punctuated by seaside outings. Evelyn now lived in a world of Deaf sisters. Just a few years older than her was Frances, 'Girl 719', who took Evelyn under her wing. Learning to talk on her hands began to complete Evelyn's language puzzle; now the missing pieces were home and Father.

Everyone in her hearing world, even Leighton, always wanted her to speak like them, where people, objects and thoughts had matching word shapes and sounds. Leighton would hold her cheeks, look her in the eye and shape the word E-V-I-E. He would stretch his mouth wide for 'E' and bite his lip for 'V', a slow smile for 'IE'. But once she was in touch with her language and culture, there was no going back.

Sign language required time and opportunity to master, and living in the country made that difficult for the Lloyd family. Stepping across two worlds of language, culture, identity and expectations began on that first day for Evelyn – the Deaf experience had its own voice, and that is what Arthur understood.

Evelyn soon learned that fingers could sign and spell, and that this was talking. The five vowels belonged at the end of each finger. The thumb was the starting point for A-E-I-O, finishing on the little finger with U. Language came from interchanging hand signs, such as thumb and forefinger opening at the mouth for 'bird' (much like her father had done), stroking the hand for 'cat' and patting the leg for 'dog'. When the twenty-six letters of the alphabet all joined together, a world of words and meanings were created.

Through close attention, Evelyn quickly mastered sign language. She could recognise and spell the short and long versions of her own name. The mouth-shape of her name was easy for her to read (at home it was said so often) – hers was a rhythmical name whether it was signed, shaped or spoken.

At school, she learned the names of other people by combining letters. She learned how to sign the numbers, initials and names of her friends, siblings and relatives. The simple signs for 'mother', 'father', 'brother' and 'sister' were also part of her early learning. She could finally match names to people, animals, objects, actions and places. Each progression held strategies, patterns, images, shapes, rhythms, riddles and surprises. The signposts of language in Evelyn's new world were obvious to her, and with every new step she took, she found her way forward.

When night ghosts visited, Evelyn could see the shape of her father. Although she had learned a lot, there was not enough language to ask when – or if – he would return. She often imagined him walking through the etched-glass doors, picking her up in his arms, taking her outside to the horse and buggy and spending another three days together, just the two of them. She dreamed of being with her father by the river, where they would see the shapes of angel feet on the sandy shore and once again bear witness to the surprise of a swimming platypus.

When she saw her father again, she would point to things and teach him her new words. He was the only person in her family who knew what her new place looked like to the outside world, although he had not yet been up the stairs to see her dormitory.

Daytime routines reminded Evelyn of her two places of belonging and separation. Just as it was for all the other children, Deaf lives were dictated by circumstances and the educational laws of the land.

Although Evelyn learned the signs for 'disappointed', 'frightened', 'upset' and 'angry', some emotions were beyond words. L-O-S-S was simple to spell, but far too difficult to explain in any language.

Though she was immersed in the world of talking on her hands, she could not yet read. Even if someone had thought to show her the announcements that appeared in the *Wangaratta Chronicle* and the Melbourne newspaper, the *Argus*, she would not have understood. Distance and deafness denied her an explanation of the loss of her God and hero.

DEATH NOTICE
ARTHUR LESLIE LLOYD
November 1923

> The regrettable demise of Mr Arthur Lloyd, of Bobinawarrah, brings back to the memory the historical fact that his father and his uncle,

> together with the late Messrs Montgomery, Brown and Simpson, the members of the noted "Farmers Five", crossed the Ovens [River] at Wangaratta on Christmas day 1857. The pioneers took up land at Bobinawarrah where they spent the remainder of their days. The house now occupied by Mr. Chas. Lloyd was built well over 60 years ago. Many descendants of the "Farmers Five" were in the large cortege on Friday.
>
> Several of the late Mr A. Lloyd's neighbours have decided to combine in a working bee at the end of this week for the purpose of taking off 35 acres of the oaten crop – a graceful, sympathetic and commendable act.
>
> Mr Arthur Lloyd died after a long illness. His death in the prime of his life is lamentable. He filled the offices of Vestryman and Representative on the College Council with conspicuous success. His ever-ready help and advice will be sadly missed.

***

At the time of Arthur's death, Evelyn was only six years old. Seven months had passed since their trip together. Now, unbeknownst to her, she would never see him again, and no-one knew how to tell her.

Adeline would often blurt out, 'Who will Evelyn tell when she's missing us?'

But not even Adeline dared to voice how Evelyn would feel when she came home and there was no Father.

Evelyn stayed at school. Reports from the Institution said she was settled, so the funeral took place without her present. In his last will and testament, Arthur provided three hundred pounds for Evelyn, more than the two hundred pounds each bequeathed to Gwen and Adeline. The Lloyd sons inherited the farm with Joey in charge, so long as she did not marry again.

Arthur Lloyd had done his duty, to himself, God and country; he had delivered Evelyn to her language and provided for his family the best way he could. Six fatherless children, aged between one and thirteen years old; the man they had all loved and relied upon was gone.

24. SOMEONE MISSING

A century has passed since Evelyn returned to her place of belonging for the first time after her father's death. I can only imagine how difficult it was for Joey when she wanted to explain moments in time to Evelyn. For me, there was always a sense of soft, shadowy silences in between what my grandmother did and did not say.

Changes took place, each day turned up with new challenges and they all did their best. Evelyn's school fees needed to be found, though the school waived them the year Arthur died. From there, they managed the following annual fees, often with Grandfather Wellington's help.

There was no opportunity for Joey to blaspheme at God, at Arthur or at how life was turning out. She worried about her own death and what would happen if she also died before all her children were independent. Her children would stay around the Oxley Shire, but it would be impossible to make that work for Evelyn. The city was where Evelyn belonged, something else Arthur was right about.

What if she had broken her promise to collect Evelyn from the deaf school? How would Arthur have explained her mother's absence to Evelyn? Joey told me that it would have been easier for him to take on that unbearable task. His presence would have been enough. But that's not how things turned out.

***

Arthur's sister Ethel often took Evelyn home to Camberwell for weekends and holidays. She wrote letters to Joey about Evelyn, 'still quiet, well-behaved and shy'. On her first return trip home, Auntie Ethel and the Dixon cousins accompanied Evelyn on the train to Wangaratta. Always firm friends, Joey trusted her sister-in-law with Evelyn's wellbeing. The very least Ethel felt she could do was look after Evelyn, since nothing would bring Arthur back.

Meanwhile, farm mornings had a tender way of announcing the ones who were missing. Remembered were the first sleepy moments when Evelyn had pattered into the kitchen, a shy smile and wave to each parent and sibling. Father's arms would lift her up high, and the queen of their castle would smile upon them all. Ensconced on Father's knee was when breakfast and the day would begin.

Evelyn's first visit home after Arthur's death was a testing time for them all. The other children had been part of the bereavement process: seeing Father in his final stages, helping with his care, saying personal goodbyes, attending the funeral, being involved in the Bobinawarrah Working Bee, going to school and helping run the farm. Joey's family were always helpful, as were Arthur's, but feeling grateful was wearing her out.

These holidays, cousins would be coming and going. Ethel and her children would be staying at Tarramia.

And Joey hoped that would be enough for Evelyn, along with being at home with her siblings.

Another easy child for Joey to manage was little Evan. He was now old enough to be interested in his watchful sister. Evelyn was delighted by a younger, sensitive brother who wanted to follow her everywhere.

Phillipa turned up and the household felt more settled with her around.

'Evelyn's home, Joey. You can rest easy now,' Phillipa said.

'It's her first time without Arthur here.'

'Yes, I know how hard that must be for—'

'That jolly man, he spoiled her rotten,' Joey snapped.

'He loved her, Joey,' Phillipa replied.

'And you think I don't?'

'No-one thinks that.'

'It's too much, the way that child followed her father's every move.'

'Yes, she did. She'll be confused until she settles in.'

'Whenever I think of Evelyn's little face, it just makes me want to cry.'

'We all feel that, Joey. No-one likes her being so far away.'

'I hate it!' Joey rarely snapped at Phillipa.

'Evelyn's home, and we all have to make her feel safe, even without Arthur here.'

'I have to keep the other children going, and I don't know who they miss the most, Arthur or Evelyn.'

'They're good children, they'll take care of Evelyn as they always have.'

'But Evelyn was so dependent on Arthur.'

'Take your time with her, Joey.'

'She won't let me, she's always preferred Arthur.'

'No, Joey. I've seen the way she looks at you.'

'Don't be silly. Evelyn loves everybody.'

'She does, but she's yours and nothing changes that.'

'If only we knew what she was thinking and could understand what she knows,' Joey said

'Don't you worry, Joey. She knows a lot more than you think,' Phillipa reassured her.

'And that's something else to worry about.'

With nothing more to say, they lifted their aprons and wiped their eyes.

***

Nearly a year had passed since that first farewell. And not one person had a clear idea about what had happened for Evelyn.

The girls at school had signed how holidays worked: 'Stay long time school, stay small time home with family.'

Evelyn had signed, 'Me happy see my family.'

'Home hard, when family can't sign.'

'My family might learn.' Evelyn hoped one of them would.

'Hard, not enough time learn,' Frances signed.

'Me learn quick,' Evelyn signed back.

'Because you have to,' Frances signed.

'Me not think.'

'Not worry. Happy home, happy come back,' Frances signed. She was older and knew how the crossing between home and school worked.

***

Home now, she'd grown and so had her siblings. Mother looked emptied out. There were so many questions to ask and so much to tell. Talking on her hands helped her to make sense of herself. Two realisations for Evelyn: at home she missed her friends, and at school she missed her family. Inside the kitchen was an apple pie cooling on the table – her favourite food and also Father's. Mother kept looking away and Auntie Phillipa would touch her gently. But they were both watching her closely.

Evelyn traced her hand over the smooth wooden arms of Father's chair. She rubbed her nose along the wood; confused, she looked towards her mother.

Mother's mouth was moving, 'Phillipa, why is she rubbing her nose over Arthur's chair?'

'Joey, I think she's trying to capture Arthur's smell.'

'Oh no, she wouldn't.'

'Yes, she would. You know how she responds to smell.'

'Philly, I don't think I've ever felt so helpless in all my life. I wish ... I just wish she would throw a tantrum or at least cry.'

'The other children will be back soon.'

'Nothing could make this right for that poor child, and I don't want to hear you or anyone else say, "Time will heal".'

Phillipa wouldn't dare.

***

Evelyn wandered outside. The house still smelled of her siblings and home, but strangely not of her father. She went to the washhouse, to the back gate where the loyal dog was pleased to see her, looked out to the paddocks and even went behind the sheds. Inside the stable was the same horse and buggy, there was still the possibility that her father must be somewhere close by.

No-one noticed when she returned inside and slipped into the dining room. The two portraits were still side by side, her and Father framed in a time before the trip to Melbourne. There he was, the man of river rides, open arms, smiling mouth, brown hair, big ears, kind eyes, soft touches, safe knees and earthy smells. Her only eyewitness between home and school.

Daylight diminished and dusk arrived. The orange-warm kitchen smelled of dinner cooking. Auntie Phillipa had left, leaving only her, Evan and Mother now. Evelyn stood at the kitchen door and waited. Suddenly, her people manifested into their individual shapes as familiar arms opened wide and came running towards her.

Leighton ran to her first, shouting, 'Evie, Evie, Evie! Here you are, home at last.'

'Lambie, you're back!' Gwen picked her up and hugged and kissed her.

'Give me a turn,' Adeline shouted at them all.

'Hello, Evelyn. Good to have you home,' Cliff said. He touched her hair, which was now in two plaits.

Little Evan pointed and said, 'Evelyn's my big sister.' And everyone wondered how a shy little boy managed such a big sentence.

'Dinner's ready,' Joey called.

Together for seven weeks under the same roof. Six familiar faces, six heartbeats all watched Evelyn as she stared at Cliff sitting in Father's chair.

Everyone held their breath, hoped she would cry, bang the table or stamp her feet, but she didn't. Instead, she looked bewildered and betrayed, and that was too much for anybody to bear.

25. SIBLING DIFFERENCE

At her school, other people began to take the place of Father and family. Evelyn met her best friend, Marge Sandon ('Girl 726'), and that meeting began a lifelong friendship for the two young deaf girls.

Evelyn and Marge slept side by side in their iron beds, and talked and laughed each night until the lights went out. Daytime hours were filled with multiple conversations happening all at once; everyone talked on their hands and interrupting each other was part of life. Language was too passionate to wait for everyone to catch up.

Developing their own language of trust and humour, Evelyn and Marge laughed easily and often. Adults were fair game and their stout matron was no exception. The little girls would hide behind the bushes to imitate her in the way they knew best – a plump person was the clawing of hands, puffed cheeks, popping eyes and a waddling walk. While it was fun, the girls would continue the story with a thumb up for 'good' and an index finger waved near the eye for 'teacher'. They knew that the matron was a 'good teacher', and that was the important part.

With three Deaf children in her family, Marge's first language was sign. Her older brother Fred was 'Boy 595' and her older sister Edna was 'Girl 698'. Evelyn had no-one in her family similar to her; a blind uncle didn't count. Next to sign language, Evelyn's greatest discovery was that some children had deaf siblings. An even bigger surprise to her was that some children had deaf parents, grandparents and other relatives.

Still, the three deaf Sandon siblings were different from each other. Marge had thick, flyaway, curly, sandy-ginger hair and soft freckles, while Edna had dark hair and looked more like their brother Fred. Marge did have the same colouring as her older brother Bill, but that was all they had in common; he was the only hearing sibling in their family. Bill, in a sense, was like Evelyn; he was the one left out of a shared sibling language. The Sandon parents were also hearing, but they had learned rudimentary signs to communicate with their three deaf children whenever they returned home.

Marge and her siblings were lucky because they were able to visit their family each weekend by catching a tram and a train; they lived near the beach, only an hour away from the city. The three Sandon siblings travelled without the help of adults, but they had each other if something went wrong. At school, Evelyn had many other friends, so talking on her hands did not stop when Marge was away; that only happened when she went back home to her family or visited the Dixons in Camberwell.

Evelyn understood that her relatives were the people she saw when she returned to Wangaratta. She wasn't related to Fred, Edna or Marge, but she discovered that when children shared deaf difference it was another way to be a brother or sister.

She would have felt less solitary at home if she could talk on her hands with at least one person, rather than always having to wait until somebody was ready for her. Girl 735 imagined having a deaf sibling. Together, they could have followed the stepping stones of their own culture and language, just like the Sandon siblings.

If only Leighton had been like Fred, she would have had her own deaf brother at school and they would have looked out for each other, and travelled on the train home together while talking on their hands about school and how much they wanted to see their family again. Evelyn did not wish for a deaf sister as well; hers were too busy helping around the farm and mothering her. But a deaf brother would have meant she was not the only child of difference in the family. Evelyn thought that Leighton could easily have crossed over into the Deaf world; he observed body language, understood ideas bigger than himself and was good at mime.

Although a 'deaf and dumb' Leighton would have upset Joey, Evelyn knew her schoolfriends would have loved him. Every day, she could have pointed to her chest for 'my', rubbed her two knuckles together for 'brother', and taken her index finger to her ear and mouth to proudly inform everyone that Leighton was 'my brother, deaf dumb'.

26. HOLIDAYS

After being accompanied on previous train trips home, these school holidays Evelyn would be travelling back to the farm alone. Her family was always happy to see her and how she had grown, but she still wished they lived closer. It was difficult to explain that to anyone, even Marge.

Evelyn thought back to all those conversations she couldn't share with her family, and remembered what she had told Marge back at school after that first trip home.

'Funny, my mother always looks sad.'

'Why you think?' Marge had asked.

'Not know, me think because no father.'

'Me think you right.'

'Make me sad.'

'Best forget.'

'Me can't.'

'You not cry.'

'Me cry when in bed, when no-one there.'

'You have many friends here,' reassured Marge.

'Good, have my friends talk same me.'

'You see family when holidays.'

'Always happy see me.'

'Your friends here, always happy see you come back.'

'Hard to know what best place.'

'Where you can talk, best place for you,' Marge reminded her.

'Me know, my father know too.'

***

School holidays were constantly talked about among the children. There was a hostel for the children who wouldn't be going home, as some families couldn't cope. But travelling home alone would show everyone that Evelyn had grown more confident.

On the day of the significant journey, one of the female teachers strode into the dormitory. As the morning light outlined the teacher's silhouette, Evelyn saw that it was her best teacher who was looking her way and signing.

'You,' pointed the teacher.

'Me?' Evelyn pointed to her own chest.

'Girl 735.'

Evelyn watched and waited.

'Today, train, go home. Me back soon.' Her hands told Evelyn.

Home was where Evelyn could then see herself. She knew the teacher would be back for her soon but she was ready, her brown suitcase was packed. The whole dormitory knew what was taking place because Deaf children never whispered in private. Conversations were available to anyone who wanted to watch or interrupt. Language had its own unique structure that was understood by everyone.

'My,' Evelyn signed.

'What?' Marge asked.

'Best teacher.'

'What do?'

'Take me train.'

'Why?'

'Me go home.'

'When?'

'Today.'

'Holidays, now me know, stupid me,' Marge signed, then giggled.

Evelyn had turned eight. This would be her first trip home unaccompanied. Her teacher was responsible for taking Evelyn on the tram to the station so that Evelyn could catch the Wangaratta train back to her family.

'You ready? Go soon,' the teacher signed as she came back into the dormitory.

'Me ready,' Evelyn replied with quiet confidence.

Talking filled the dormitory. 'Have good time,' came from a flurry of little girls' hands.

'Me miss you,' Marge said.

'Me see you when holiday finish.' Evelyn could now see both sides of her own future.

Going home for Evelyn still meant no Father, but most days at home she would tiptoe into the dining room to look up at the two grand portraits of her and her father on the wall of the front room. Beside Mother's bed was always the small photo of him in his army uniform looking proud, kind and true, just as Evelyn remembered him. The photo stayed there until the family sold the farm, and then Joey tucked it away somewhere.

Changes took place, each day turned up with new

challenges, and they all did their best. The farm required full commitment from every family member. Having Evelyn back home was an adjustment, although they were happier having her with them. For Joey, having Evelyn home was a relief and a guilt-ridden reminder of how far away her daughter was in distance, language and culture. When it came time to communicate, they all had their own basic language of pointing and showing, and she was included in most things. But despite their love and good intentions, they were all pleased that she could amuse herself.

***

Steam trains shuddered as they waited for Evelyn and other deaf children to catch them to different country destinations. Though they were not on her train, Marge had told Evelyn about the Hately brothers, older boys who caught the train home to Camperdown by themselves, and their hearing mother who would be waiting for them at the station. Marge had signed that although Mrs Hately had nine children, she had learned basic signs to communicate with her deaf sons.

Some parents learned sign language, some attempted to learn basic signs and some were too ashamed of their deaf children to even try. The Lloyd family were not ashamed of Evelyn, but it would take time for them to learn sign language, and would be quickly forgotten without regular practice. The complexities of any language would take time and patience. Although sign language looked obvious, it was more intricate than people might expect. Joey did not need something as important as sign language to make her feel like a failure; she always felt that she was letting Evelyn down somehow.

Train journeys had rhythm and repetition, and linked Evelyn to Melbourne, home, family, doctors, relatives, friends and school. Deaf children were always seated in convenient compartments that allowed them to easily see their home stations and whoever would be waiting to greet them.

High steps, her teacher's hand, train smells, familiar vibrations, honey-coloured wood and the out-of-reach water fountain near the doorway all signified the beginning of her journey home. Smoke eclipsed the billowing sky as Evelyn's thoughts went back to her schoolfriends. Now she knew what was missing – time away from language and culture could only withstand the length of a holiday.

The teacher whispered to the conductor, 'This child is deaf and dumb. Here's her ticket to Wangaratta. Her family will be waiting for her at the station. Can you please make sure she is placed in a carriage with some women?'

'I'll take care of it, Missus. There's one with ladies going all the way to Wang.'

'What man say?' Evelyn asked.

'Lady look after you,' the teacher reassured Evelyn.

Then reassurance for the conductor and herself. 'She's a very good child and will be no bother.'

'Don't worry, Missus, I'll pop in and have a look at her later.'

'Thank you.'

'Man look after you.' The teacher's hands told Evelyn.

Inside the carriage, Evelyn's brown leather case and a

small box of Institution food was placed on the brass rack. High up – too high – she would never step on the train seat, although she knew some Deaf children, boys mainly, who would.

Evelyn was such an appealing child that train travellers were always willing to help. She watched her teacher hand the pink ticket to the conductor before turning back to her.

'You happy go home?' the teacher signed.

Evelyn gave the teacher a shy nod in reply.

'All good, you have happy time with family.'

'Thank you.'

Smoky Spencer Street Station, red train carriages and the big black engine made her first time travelling alone feel a little less intimidating. She was on her way. Evelyn would only know everything was alright when she arrived at Wangaratta Station, travelled down the road through Milawa to Bobinawarrah and could see, smell and touch each one of her people.

Images of the farm and the taste of home-cooked food came to her. Her mother would have fresh bread, jam and cream, cakes, and fruit and vegetables picked from the garden. Gwen would be cooking something delicious; her big sister knew what food she liked. A special surprise would be Auntie Phillipa's shortbreads.

Others on the train looked at the little girl with the shy smile who could sit still for a very long time staring into faces and places. She could sum people up with one glance, but what they didn't know was that her moving fingers were spelling invisible words. Her language world had expanded and she was keen to share her newfound knowledge.

Evelyn looked out the window as she pictured words to teach Leighton on her return. She would use visual spaces, signs and shapes. L-E-I-G-H-T-O-N was a long name, no repeat letters. No more signing 'best brother boy' – her hands could now spell his name.

A black-hatted woman, shaping her mouth in loud and exaggerated pronunciation, was talking to her.

'Child, are you frightened? There's nothing to be afraid of. You will see your mother soon.'

The woman used overinflated mouth shapes like her cousin Vaughan, foolish and comical but not unkind. Last holidays, Leighton had learned some sign words from her; he was always ready to learn her language. They would work together on the more difficult aspects of communication, like they always had.

Melbourne was the place where Evelyn was not always the last to know. Her school report showed that her reading and writing skills were developing alongside her signing: 'Education good. Conduct excellent. Speech quite good (inferiority complex). Encouragement would draw her out.' The remarks were a welcome change for Joey, who had barely recovered from the words on Evelyn's school registration papers, which had come to her after Arthur passed away. 'Not an imbecile,' they had stated, and Joey didn't know whether to be pleased or devasted.

During this visit, her family would have paper and pencils at hand and she'd now be able to write notes for them. For them to learn sign language would be a road too far; time was too fragmented when they never knew what would happen next.

Evelyn's homecoming was always complete when she could see one or more of her people waiting for her on the platform. When she looked through the window, she hoped to see her favourite brother waving and running alongside the train as it pulled into the station, his mouth shaping, 'Evie ... Evie ... Evie.'

27. ABSENCE

Joey was the only Wellington child given just one Christian name, but during the last few years she had reluctantly acquired a middle one: absence. The number of people missing from her world was mounting up and Joey did not want to keep counting. But there were two she could still locate: Emmeline in South Africa and Evelyn in Melbourne.

Over the last two years, nothing much had gone right for Joey. She knew it was her responsibility to follow Evelyn's education; Arthur had expected that of her. But life would not stop long enough for Joey to catch up. All she could do was keep moving forward and do what must be done. God's gifts could not be explained to herself, let alone to any of her children.

When Evelyn arrived at Wangaratta Station, it was empty of her people until she saw her grandparents hurrying up the platform, and they took her home to the farm in their car.

Her grandparents took her inside through the back door, and her suitcase was placed on the floor inside the familiar kitchen. Evelyn could smell food, wood, clothes and family. But there was a stillness that dominated, another absent presence. Mother and sisters moved to her, wanted to hold her, but she would not be held by anyone until she found her favourite brother.

Absent smells and spaces already belonged to Father. His empty space stayed alive inside their shared three-day journey and river language. And his portrait was still side by side with hers in the dining room. Home and farm spaces were filled by her family, until one of them went missing. And, of course, there was always Leighton. He would never leave her; he needed her as much as she needed him, and Mother found peace with Leighton in the room.

When Evelyn was away, her quiet time was the darkness of school bedtime. She would hold the shape of her family between both hands, the way she had witnessed her siblings saying their evening prayers. Each night before she fell asleep, she would see her family slip into their familiar places on the farm.

On this return, the dog was in his place, but he looked too sad to say hello. The sheds, buggies, horses, chickens, gardens and orchards were all the same, but not all her people were where she had left them.

'Whatever is that child doing?' Joey asked.

'I think she's looking for Leighton,' Gwen said.

'It's too much.'

'Can you imagine how it must be for her? Father had told her he would pick her up from school and never did, and now ...'

'Oh, Gwen, she didn't hear what Father said.'

'He told *us*, though, remember?'

'Yes, yes, I know he said that. Many things have been said and never followed through.'

'She might not have heard it, but she would have

expected him to come back. He never left her alone for a minute.' Gwen understood Evelyn's patterns of behaviour. She yearned to tell Lambie that she missed their father too.

'We all have to get used to things, Gwen, even Evelyn.'

Gwen knew that this time her Lambie deserved an explanation, but it was one more thing that this young teenage girl was not yet old enough to manage.

'Mother, how can you say that?' Gwen said.

'Well, we have to. And the quicker the better, I say.' Joey was too sad to even try and understand her life. She had nothing left over to accept God's latest decision.

Her beautiful boy – creative, intuitive, strong and healthy – was gone.

One night, he complained of stomach pains. Joey had put him to bed thinking he had overeaten, although that was something he had never done before. Something else hard to forgive – Joey knew that her children never complained.

Unbearable moaning went on all night. Only little Evan had slept. Before the sun rose, Joey could wait no longer.

'Cliff, ride the horse over to Uncle Charlie's. Tell him to come quickly with the horse and buggy. We'll have to take Leighton to hospital in town.'

Uncle Charlie came alone so there would be enough room for Leighton to lie flat and for Joey to reach her boy from the front seat. Auntie Phillipa would come across as soon as she could get a lift. Joey, Gwen and Adeline hadn't left Leighton's side all night, but they would not all fit in the buggy. In any case, someone would have to stay behind to take care of three-year-old Evan and do the milking. More blankets were added, but the boy was too hot to be covered, even on a cold May morning.

'Charlie, I don't think I can take any more.'

'Joey, he'll be alright. It's probably his appendix, and they can take that out in town. We'll find out what's wrong and he'll be as right as rain in a week or so.'

The journey from Bobinawarrah to Westham Hospital on the corner of Green and Rowan streets took well over an hour of slow, rough riding. Dr W. Browne was on duty on 25 May 1925. He took Leighton into the surgery, but it was not appendicitis. The boy had a twisted bowel, and there was no place in Wangaratta that was equipped to do an operation to help him. Melbourne was the only chance, and that was more than seven hours away in the fastest car.

Joey sat with her boy for the two hours and fifteen minutes it took for him to die. Nothing could save him, despite how much she loved him. Leighton Wellington Lloyd was twelve years and eleven months old when he died, not even a teenager.

She had not had enough time to prepare herself for Leighton's death in the way she had for Arthur's. Someone organised her children and the funeral. Somehow Joey kept moving, one foot in front of the other.

Leighton was buried at Milawa Cemetery on 29 May 1925, in the same grave as his father and close to other family members. The death certificate noted the official cause of death as 'Volvulus Acute Intestinal Obstruction'.

Someone rang the Institution. It was agreed that Evelyn should be told this time. She was older and had access to more language that would explain things to her.

***

My mother was told of her brother's death via a phone call to the Institution. I know this because when I began trying to understand my mother's Deaf experience, I asked her what had happened when people died in her family, and how she had found out. She told me the following story.

One rainy day in May 1925, during her third year at the Deaf school, Evelyn was sick in bed in the dormitory. An older girl came up to her and pointed to Evelyn for 'your', rubbed her two knuckles together for 'brother' and spread her two hands out at the shoulders for 'dead'. They had put a Deaf child in charge of explaining to Evelyn 'your brother dead'.

Sign language can be a blunt tool of communication. A dormitory in an institution was not like being at home, where she would have been able to skim-read those around her to understand what would happen next. Her aunts and sisters would have been of comfort to her.

Left alone to process this strange information, Evelyn was puzzled. Which brother? When her father hadn't returned, there had been no older girl, no explanation, no siblings, no farm and not enough language at that stage to help her understand. Early on, she had only had simple words, like 'me', 'apple', 'bed', 'book', 'bath', 'wash', 'school', 'dress', 'play' and 'friend'. Practical, useful words for actions, people and objects – nothing to explain emotions or loss. Even later, it felt like there would never be enough signs for her feelings, And there was no-one there to help her learn how to manage all those feelings.

I signed to my mother, 'What you do?' She answered with signs, words and feelings that I will never forget.

'Cry' in sign language is a sad expression and both index

fingers trailing down the cheeks. 'Me cry and cry.'

Evelyn cried when she found out her brother had died, but she didn't know which brother she was crying for. She had three brothers back home on the farm. She could spell their names on her hands: C-L-I-F-F, L-E-I-G-H-T-O-N and E-V-A-N, or sign 'big', 'best' or 'baby brother'. Evelyn had learned which name belonged to each brother. L-E-I-G-H-T-O-N was the longest and hardest to spell, but the most important name was worth her commitment.

My mother told me that a teacher brought her some food and left it for her to eat or ignore. Alone in a dormitory of twenty-five empty beds, she grieved for her dead brother, not knowing which brother had died – or gone missing, as she had come to think of it. She hoped it wasn't her very best brother, L-E-I-G-H-T-O-N. Her very best brother and friend.

Newspaper obituaries were cut out and kept. When she was older, she could read how Leighton was the 'loving brother' of all his siblings. Evelyn became the fourth and not the fifth name in the family, although she and her brothers and sisters would each always be one of six siblings. That was who they were.

The Argus

Saturday 6 June 1925

> LLOYD.— On the 28th May, at Westham private hospital, Wangaratta, Leighton Wellington, second son of Josephine and the late Arthur Lloyd, of Bobinawarrah, and loving brother of Clifton, Gwenllian, Adeline, Evelyn and Evan, aged 12 years and 11 months.

After my mother told me this story, I remember going to my bedroom and crying. I was about the same age as she had been when she found out. For me, learning that Evelyn's deafness excluded her from sharing in family grief was a harsh realisation of what some parts of life had meant for a 'deaf and dumb' child.

Leighton was rarely mentioned as I was growing up, although Joey would tell me about him whenever I thought to ask. She loved to talk about her son's eye for detail, his sense of wonder, his free spirit. That's how I found out that he loved the theatre of church, festive flowers, story-filled shop windows, beautiful clothes and attending to his tiny sister. It's also how I learned that Leighton was the only one who ever called my mother 'Evie'. Leighton became another story of silence and not enough questions asked, a reminder that the Lloyd family knew how to keep grief to themselves.

Leighton Wellington Lloyd can never be forgotten. To this very day, the original house and property are there in Bobinawarrah, and the front gate has the cursive script that announces that the farm is still called 'Leighton'.

Josephine (Wellington) and Arthur Leslie Lloyd on their wedding day, 23 January 1908 at Saint Matthews Church of England, Albury, NSW.

The Lloyd family at Bobinawarrah: Joey holding baby Evelyn, Gwenllian seated, Clifton standing, Arthur seated, Adeline at his feet and Leighton seated in front of Evelyn and Joey.

Right: Evelyn, age three, with Adeline in the background.

Below: The Wellington and Lloyd families: Evelyn (about fourteen years old) with plaits, kneeling in the front row; Evan on her right, Grandfather Wellington behind her; Joey on her left shoulder; Adeline kneeling second from the left in the front row; and Cliff with the boy on his knee.

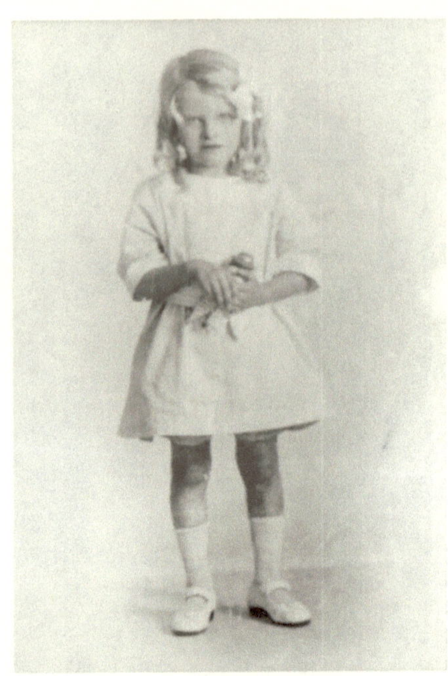

Left: Portrait of four-year-old Evelyn after her Melbourne diagnosis, 1921.

Below: The Victorian Deaf and Dumb Institution in 1923, Eve's first year. Eve is in the front row, second from the left. Art is on the end (right side) of the second back row.

Top: Eve and Art's wedding day, 2 October 1942.

Bottom, left: Eve and Art with Dawn (six weeks old) in Phillips Street, Coburg.

Bottom, right: Eve, Art and Dawn in Melbourne, May 1945.

Above: Eve and Dawn (second from left) with Deaf mothers and their children, in 1945, on the lawn in front of the interdenominational chapel (built in 1930 for the Deaf); Jolimont Square, East Melbourne.

Opposite: Living in Carrum, Dawn (at eighteen months) riding the horse that Art built.

Above: Dawn and Lloyd off to the city with our father to see our first Charlie Chaplin film.

Clockwise from top left on opposite page: Home from the farm and pointing out the future to my new baby brother, Lloyd, 1947.

Lloyd 'Ned' Hately and his old hat after the move to Bonbeach.

Art holding Dawn, Eve holding Lloyd, 1947.

Above: Evan's wedding on 1 March 1952, the Lloyd family together.
Back row: Clifton, Evelyn, Adeline, Evan.
Front row: Gwenllian and Josephine.

Opposite, top: Carrum, 8 August 1948. Deaf and hearing mothers and children at Dawn's fourth birthday party. Marjorie Parker, top left, wearing a striped jumper and apron; Evelyn standing near her, seven months pregnant with Valerie; blond Lloyd in the back row; Dawn, centre front with two hair ribbons and a frown; Gary Parker behind her.

Opposite, bottom: Eve and Art's five children from left to right; Valerie, Wendy, Dawn, Lloyd and Karen, 1955.

PART TWO

… like everyone else I am what I am: an individual, unique and different, with a lineal history of ancestral promptings and urgings; a history of dreams, desires, and of special experiences, all of which I am the sum total.

– Charlie Chaplin, *My Autobiography*

28. DEAF BELONGING

Boy 587 first crossed paths with Girl 735 at the Victorian Deaf and Dumb Institution. When revisiting their school photograph in 1923, the future would have been impossible to predict. Angelic Evelyn, six years old, is seated in the front row, second from the left. Several rows behind, standing tall, is bespectacled teenager Arthur Edward Hately.

Known as Eve and Art in the Deaf world (although she was always Evelyn to her family), he was the serious one and she was the sporty one. After they each left school at age sixteen, their Deaf world was work, picnics, beach visits, parties, socials, sport, billiards, chess and the Deaf Club. Photographs of Eve show her with handsome men, or as part of the various social groups of their world. Art was involved in different committees for Deaf welfare, education and social events. Socialising was also a big part of his Deaf connections.

In those days, most people paired off by their late twenties or so, and, at the ages of thirty-three and twenty-five respectively, so did Art and Eve.

When I was growing up, my father was my guru on the language of life. My relentless pursuit of people and places comes from him – he wanted me to live in both the hearing and Deaf worlds. As a native signer, I understood without being told how sign language used hand movements, sign order, and body and facial cues to communicate. There was a grammar and syntax in the language that I spoke with my parents that had different patterns from that of the hearing world. Missing words did not change the meaning of what they wanted to say, but they could interrupt sense and flow for someone who had little experience of the structure of sign language.

Still, the language of love had its own voice. There was a story I liked my father to tell me over and over again. E-V-E is what he would sign for this story, never 'mother' or 'mum'.

'Tell me when you see Mum at Deaf Club.'

'Again? You know story.'

'Me want know again.'

'When Eve walk into Deaf Club, everyone stop see what wearing.'

'Her look beautiful?'

'Always wear different clothes.'

He would smile in the telling, proud of her point of difference, and his own for being clever enough to notice. Without saying so, we both agreed that he had married the most attractive woman at the Deaf Club, and the one who happened to be my pretty mother.

I never asked my mother what she thought of my father, a man of many contradictions and passions. I assumed she would agree with me that he was something better than handsome, an interesting-looking man who people thought was also clever. And that was what he wanted them to think, too – that he was a clever man despite his deafness.

My parents were probably surprised to be married to each other. Eve was attractive, lively, fun and kind, and everyone loved her, while Art was intense, an observer of the world around him and also a bit of a snob about what he knew. Eve was a catch – family and friends knew it and, fortunately, so did Art. Their world was a balancing act of differences, love, language and belonging.

29. EVE AND ART

Evelyn Ida Lloyd and Arthur Edward Hately were married at midday on 2 October 1942 at the Deaf community's Mediterranean-style, non-denominational church, with refreshments afterwards at the Deaf and Dumb Society on Wellington Parade in Jolimont (now known as Expression Australia). This was one celebration where the Deaf outnumbered the hearing.

The wartime wedding did not allow for a traditional bridal gown, but Eve's knee-length, soft-blue crepe dress was a neat fit for her slim body and she wore a bold corsage instead of carrying a bouquet. Her black straw hat had a perky tilt and a small veil, and beneath it her hair was coiffured into ringlets. It was an expensive hat, but too harsh for her soft features.

'Hate hat,' she stamped at her mother. But the hat could not be changed on the morning of the wedding. Joey had paid for the whole outfit, as well as the reception refreshments; she felt she was always paying for Evelyn in some way.

Joey was dressed to the nines and nothing – not even the relentless challenges of her life – would prevent her from turning up for Evelyn's wedding day. Cliff was there in his best suit, ready to be his sister's witness, but the rest of the family was either at home in Oxley Shire working, away in the RAAF or having babies.

Jean and Alan, Art's hearing parents, were also there. Art's unassuming mother always turned up to support her Deaf sons, although his square-jawed father shuffled with unspoken discomfort. Like Joey, he was unsure of what to do with Deaf difference.

The three Deaf Hately boys had each other and a strong sense of identity in a family of nine siblings. They had love and acceptance from all their sisters and their mother, though I'm not so sure about their father or their one hearing brother. But in the Hately family, they all had someone like them.

The attractive and popular couple shared friends, language and culture. Since leaving the farm, Eve had spent most of her time in the Deaf world. Although she returned home to Joey and her siblings occasionally, she belonged with her own language and culture. Eve's wellbeing was still her family's highest priority, and Joey and the Lloyd family did take to Art. In their eyes, for a 'deaf and dumb' man, he seemed smart, hardworking, independent and respectful. Though he wasn't religious, and liked a beer but was not a big drinker, he, like everyone else, was smitten by Eve.

Art worked at Foy's department store as a carpenter and was a prominent member of the Deaf Club, busy on committees making decisions about other Deaf people's futures. Eve worked at the brassiere factory, and when Joey once went to the factory to visit Evelyn's supervisor, he told her, 'If you have any more girls like Evelyn, please send them to me. She is one of our best workers.'

Pride and Joey caught the train home that day, although it was a brief respite from the years she had spent worrying about Evelyn. Joey's anxiety over her daughter of difference followed her wherever she went, and continued to do so until her dying day.

During the war, there had been no honeymoon, only a tram trip to the weatherboard house on Phillips Street in West Coburg where Art lived. It was located a short distance from their jobs and their communal gathering places. Art rented rooms from the landlord and his wife, who had become familiar with the strange sounds of the Deaf. They would tell everyone, 'The deaf and dumb couple are the perfect tenants.'

The city was Eve's world, one she'd enjoyed since leaving school and starting work at sixteen. But now, as a wife, she was ready to follow her friends who were having babies.

For Art and Eve, there was much excitement and anticipation about their first baby's impending birth. There was a symbolic neatness to a birth scheduled to take place on the eighth day of the eighth month in the year of 1944.

'Eight, eight, forty-four, baby come,' Art signed.

'Baby might come early,' replied Eve.

'Good luck, birthday, right time come.'

'You think baby deaf?'

'Not matter.'

'Me hope baby can hear.'

'Good number, lucky baby.' Art had high expectations for his child.

According to Chinese astrological charts, any child with the numbers eight and four in their birthdate would be born lucky. But Eve and Art believed having children was all the good fortune they would need; they were ready to be parents. They would create their own luck and history.

Eve approached giving birth in a practical manner, and her journey towards motherhood began with a healthy pregnancy. Her Deaf friends made mothering look easy. There were few support networks in place for women then, but Deaf sisters had each other. Many of her friends were having children, and her best friend Marge already had a boy and a girl, both hearing. Other friends had only hearing children, or only deaf children, while some had both, and they all seemed to manage. Deaf women never complained about childbirth, or whether their child would be born deaf or hearing. Neither outcome was a crisis.

The parents-to-be talked on their hands all the time about their baby. They spent time choosing a name they could pronounce and sign easily, and they discussed night-time feeds, visits to the health centre, prams and cots. Wishing to be ready and organised, one sunny day Eve gently washed her hospital garments and all the baby clothes given to her by her mother, sisters, aunts and friends. Sunshine would warm the future for her child; Eve loved the sun and would be putting her baby outside every chance she could.

Although Eve's family suppressed their concerns about whether the baby would be 'unlucky enough to be born deaf and dumb', the thought never went away. They worried that a deaf child would make it harder for both Evelyn and the baby, but especially for the rest of the family. No-one stopped to consider how a deaf baby would give Eve a blood relation just like herself, and that she would never again be the odd one out in her family.

But one hearing parent – Art's gentle and quiet mother, Jean – was not at all concerned about the impending birth. She loved her three Deaf sons in the same unassuming way she loved all of her nine children, and she knew this baby already had everything it needed. Art and one of his Deaf brothers, Bill, would be fathers for the first time within weeks of each other, and although their mother didn't go to church often, she trusted in the grace of God.

My father often told me of the unheralded actions of his mother, a woman before her time. As a child, my father would tap his busy mother on the leg with questions about the world and beyond. She would stop whatever she was doing and respond to her intense and curious boy. She never overcompensated for Deaf difference, and she learned to sign so she could share in her sons' language. My father always remembered that she gave him and his Deaf brothers what they needed most: her full attention.

Both Gwen and Adeline were married with children, and either circumstance or choice had kept them in the Oxley Shire. By the time Evelyn was pregnant with her first child, Adeline already had three youngsters and Gwen had two daughters, although she had lost one child at only eighteen months old. At that time, Gwen was also early into a new pregnancy, and her baby was due to be born seven months after Evelyn's.

In stoic Joey style, family issues were never discussed in front of others. But not even a religious husband or a drinking one could ever stop the sisters turning up for each other. They came from strong Wellington women and, along with Joey, individual anxieties were bottled up and they were always there for Evelyn. Three mothers with different approaches, but all caring for the same reasons: love, guilt and responsibility.

Throughout Evelyn's pregnancy, whispers skittered around the family.

'Poor Evelyn … What if the baby is born deaf and dumb?'

While deep down they knew Evelyn would manage, there was doubt and dread about how they would relate to her children if one or more was born deaf. Evelyn had learned to talk on her hands and had shown everyone she was a popular, funny, kind, joyful and hardworking young woman. But they still worried about the possibility of a deaf baby. Eve and Art would be 'deaf and dumb' parents and, along with Art's family history, that doubled their chances of a 'deaf and dumb' baby, as far as Evelyn's family understood genetics.

'Mother, are you worried?' asked Gwen.

'God forbid that they'll have any children like them.'

'Mother, we'll deal with that if it happens, you know we will,' retorted Adeline.

'Let's just hope that it doesn't.'

***

Life beneath the Bobinawarrah sky disappeared when the farm, with the nameplate 'Leighton' on the front gate, was sold. Everyone received their allocated share according to Arthur's last will and testament, and Joey never married again. If she had, she would have lost her small inheritance. Of the brothers, good-natured Cliff was never going to be a farmer's bootlace. He had moved to Heidelberg West with his strong-willed wife from St Arnaud and their two young children. Handsome Evan had joined the RAAF, where his skills were employed to make coffins. He was forever grateful to have been saved from a farmer's life, and secretly so was Joey. She had bought a house on Melton Avenue in Carnegie, close to Melbourne. She had picked a home near the train line so it would be easy for Evelyn to visit.

Joey continued to turn up for Evelyn, and to make something from nothing with a little income on the side by letting out rooms for a number of years. She also opened a frock shop called Josephine's in Armadale. Family gossip was that Joey had affairs. I, for one, hope she did. Who could blame her? She was still a young woman when her destiny was turned on its head. In my opinion, there had to be more to life for Joey than singing in the church choir, working hard and worrying about her children. 'Poor Evelyn' still remained her main concern, now that a baby was on the way. It could have been enough for Joey that Eve and Art were content with their lives, but it never quite was.

30. FIRSTBORN

Nothing very new was taking place on a cold August evening in West Coburg in 1944. By ages thirty-five and twenty-seven respectively, and married for nearly two years, Eve and Art were unsure as to why it had taken so long for this pregnancy to happen. But they were both excited about having their own child. Boy or girl, deaf or hearing, they didn't mind – healthy and curious was their only wish.

Eve went into labour on the morning of Monday 7 August. She tapped the sleeping Art on the arm and calmly signed, 'Back pain, me think time hospital.'

Always a quick thinker, he jumped out of bed, hurried from their room and across the passageway, and knocked on their landlord's varnished brown door.

'Hang on, I'll call a taxi,' the landlord yelled back through the door. 'Bloody hell, he can't hear me,' he said to his wife, who had already turned on the light.

Art saw the light beneath the door. The Deaf plan ahead – Art and the landlord had written out a strategy for any time of day or night. The phone box was close by, the hospital was only a few streets away, so it would be just a short taxi ride to get there.

'Crikey, I hope they'll be okay,' said the landlord.

'Eve will be right as rain,' said his wife. 'I've never met such a practical woman. It's only a baby she's having, not a koala bear.'

'Well, they are deaf and dumb.'

'And what's that got to do with having a baby?'

'I guess Art always knows who to ask for help,' said the landlord.

And together, the landlord, with half his shirt buttons undone, and his wife, still in her chenille dressing gown, stood at the front gate to wave them off. Eve shyly waved back.

Babies were everywhere Eve looked, and she knew her mother and sisters would turn up when needed. Art came from an even larger family, where people had babies all the time, but neither of them knew too much about the birthing process. Art wanted Eve to be safe; once inside the hospital ward she would be on her own.

The engine of the taxi barely had time to warm up before they arrived at the front entrance of Vaucluse Hospital. Art carried the case and held Eve's arm, but she was able to walk to the main desk. It was still early in the day, so there were not many people around. Cleanliness was what Eve always noticed, and the hospital's highly polished floors and the scent of disinfectant reassured her.

'Smell clean,' she signed.

'Not long now, me back later.'

'You go, me good.' Eve was calm.

Art completed the hospital forms as Eve was whisked away. He was nervous about leaving his wife alone with no-one to speak for her, and labour pains would not allow time for written explanations. They reached another language crossroad inside the hospital, but the nursing staff seemed unfazed. They knew it was Eve's first baby, and they also knew it would be a long labour ahead for the 'deaf and dumb' woman.

Labour was another unexplained journey for Eve. There was no-one telling her everything would be alright or when to push. Her language had left the hospital with her husband, who was sent home to wait for however long the baby would take to appear. Before Art left, the matron in charge waved him over and wrote a message on his notepad: *You can come back during evening visiting hours if the baby has not arrived before then.*

Rain outside, warm hospital lights inside, the nurses spoke the language of kindness, touch and care, but not the language of sign. Eve was experienced in finding her way through silence and, for the sake of her baby, she would do what must be done. Eve never made a fuss. A gentle demeanour attracts attention in any language and she was supported in the best way possible. It would be many years before interpreters would be made freely available to Deaf patients.

That night, Art was the first to turn up for visiting hours. He arrived on the dot of 7 pm. Eve was exhausted; it had already been a long labour. She was past caring what date the baby wanted to arrive.

'Take long time,' she signed.

All Art could do was hold her hand and sign with his other hand, 'Not long, soon.'

I must have known what my parents wanted, so I arrived at 1:30 am on the eighth day of the eighth month of 1944. Eve held me and we were both bathed. We were then separated – I was taken to the nursery and Eve to the ward.

Up early, after staying awake most of the night, Art visited the hospital again on Tuesday morning without knowing whether he was a new father. He was hopeful there would be news by then, for everyone's sake. When he stopped at the nurses' station, they handed him a piece of paper that said: *A girl.*

When he reached her on the ward, he pulled back the curtains and saw a tired but happy Eve.

'Healthy girl, over seven pounds,' she signed.

'Good. You good?' Art asked. Eve was at her prettiest, even after that long night. 'Nurse tell me, can go see baby.'

'You go now, me sleep, see you tonight.'

'See you tonight, baby girl, good.' He was about to leave when Eve tapped him on the arm.

'What?'

'Not forget to tell my mother baby here.'

'Me will.' Day one of her motherhood journey and even though she was tired, Art knew she was ready.

Art was alone as he looked through the glass window of the nursery. The nurse held up a pink bundle, his new baby girl. They had already decided on a name: D-A-W-N, a one-syllable name they could both say in ways that would always be easy to recognise, whether their child was deaf or hearing. Her second name was Evelyn, Art had insisted. Dawn Evelyn Hately was the first child of two doting Deaf parents.

Following my birth, Art made sure that everyone was notified. He had a list of names and numbers and enough coins. Once again, the landlord helped my father by ringing people who would then pass on the happy news.

Art went to work, but his boss told him he could leave early. He caught a tram to the Deaf Club and posted the notice of my arrival. Deaf people passed through daily for many reasons, so the news travelled quickly through the Deaf world.

When their phone calls came through, Joey and Gwen were both pleased and relieved, but still worried for all sorts of random reasons. They tried to keep their opinions to themselves, but it was hard to keep them from each other.

After ten days in hospital, the two Deaf parents returned to Phillips Street with their new baby. Both were unconcerned; a baby with so much attention would not create obstacles. At least not that early in her life.

Joey had visited Eve and the baby in hospital, had seen she was healthy and that Eve was happy. But along with Gwen, she continued to worry, especially about what would happen when the baby cried at night. Eventually Adeline, fed up with their pessimistic comments, told them, 'Don't worry about Evelyn. There's nothing she can't do, apart from hear.'

Eve's mother and sisters did not know that plans had already been put in place, and they never thought to ask. Art had worked out how their new baby would be heard. Night feeds every four hours required a concentrated strategy.

Somehow, the landlord and Art spoke the same language. Together they worked out how a ball of string could be put to use. Each night, for as long as it would take, a length of string was tied firmly to Art's toe and then to the landlord's toe. At least it was economical; the two bedrooms were only across the hall from each other.

'How long is a piece of string?' the landlord asked his wife.

'As long as it takes for a baby to cry,' his wife bantered back.

Every time the baby woke up for a night feed, the string was pulled and Art would turn and wake Eve who would breastfeed. Then the landlord would go back to sleep until the next feed. Meanwhile, Art watched over his wife and daughter.

Pride took over for Eve. By the time her baby was six weeks old, she knew her every move. A baby who was breastfed, bathed and swaddled, and had her brow stroked to sleep had no good reason to cry. One day when Art came home from work, she signed, 'Me no want string, me always know when baby cry.' No-one knew how she did it, but it seemed that when it came to her baby, Eve had an extra sense.

There was one thing the landlord and Art worked out that they did not tell Eve. If the hall light was being switched on and off, it meant there was something wrong. But it turned out to be a plan that was not required. Guardian angels seemed to watch over every move Eve and Art's energetic daughter made, and no-one, other than Eve's family, was concerned about whether this child was deaf or hearing.

31. UNCERTAINTY

As the firstborn child in my family, everything about my world belonged inside the environment I shared with my parents. Language was in the fingertips, immediate and physical, and my life began in a tactile way with eighteen months of breastfeeding. There were never bottles or dummies; just a gentle finger rubbed on my brow or at the side of my head would soothe me to sleep. Breastfeeding covered the four senses of smell, taste, touch and sight, and there was no-one but me to know that there was also sound. My mother gave me her full attention.

I was born to be a native signer long before anyone, even my parents, knew whether I would be a native speaker. The Deaf world was never concerned about where I would belong; they had seen every configuration of family working out. But my mother's familial hearing world was always concerned that a Deaf child in the family might be another cross that they would be expected to carry.

Language bridges were a way of life in the Deaf world. Crossing over into the hearing world was the natural order of things, but it was not a two-way crossing. Long before I even knew what it meant, people would tell me, 'Aren't you lucky you weren't born deaf and dumb.' I grew up hearing these words from people who thought it was a compliment.

There were no tests available then for a new baby, other than observation. Eve and Art followed every movement I made and watched how I responded to vibrations that they knew to be sounds.

'Me know early you not deaf dumb,' my father would tell me when I asked.

'How?' I would sign.

'Me know.'

'Me always know you not deaf dumb,' my mother also signed.

My parents could sense and respond to vibrations, but their experience of the hearing world had shown them how sound was constant, subtle, absorbed and taken for granted. Hard to explain what they knew to others who had no sense of a Deaf experience.

During every visit by my mother's family, someone watched me for any signs of being 'deaf and dumb'. They had failed to recognise the early signs in Evelyn and were determined not to make the same mistake twice.

Family visits only happened a few times a year, but they were enough to show them that my mother was content. In fact, she made mothering look easier than they thought it should be for a 'deaf and dumb' woman.

'Dawn is a real livewire,' Gwen would say. Her own new baby was a placid boy, but she still grieved the loss of her firstborn child. She was relieved that things were going well for Evelyn, who would always be her very own Lambie.

'She does seem to hear everything that's going on,' replied Joey.

'She follows everything Evelyn and Art do, including any sounds they make.'

'But it's their sign language that she seems to follow most, and that worries me. If she can hear, how will she learn to talk properly?'

'Here we go again …' sighed Gwen, unwilling to take on more of Joey's anxieties.

'We can't wait until she goes to school like we did with Evelyn – that's far too long.'

'We could take her with us, but Evelyn and Art would never allow that.'

'I don't think that baby would be happy away from her mother, or her father for that matter.'

'You're right, Mother, I've never seen such an attached child. She and Evelyn are joined at the hip.'

'Who would have thought? But she will have to learn to talk.'

'Let's worry about that if we have to, Mother.'

***

Like other women of the time, Eve parked her pram outside the shops, where a sleeping or sitting baby was considered safe. Until the day she came out with her shopping to find that, although she had strapped me in, I was standing and bouncing up and down. Helpless, she watched as her strong-willed daughter upturned the pram and all her shopping.

A practical solution was needed. Never still, I was always looking for the next step and appeared ready to begin walking at ten months. On one visit, Art showed my grandmother and aunt the bricks he had placed in the bottom of the pram. He put up his hand for 'stop' and his other hand showed 'tipped over'.

That sort of sign language they both understood.

'Good grief, Gwen!' said Joey. 'And Dawn's only nine months old!'

'She'll be walking very soon, mark my words.'

'But then Evelyn won't be able to hear where the child is!'

'She'll know, Mother. Remember how she always knew how to find any one of us when she was a tiny tot?'

Before Joey could think of something else to worry about, Gwen used Auntie Phillipa's tactic and changed the subject. She pointed to the pram.

'See, Mother, Art thinks of everything. And he helps Evelyn as much as he can, not like most men.'

'At least that's one thing we don't have to worry about ... for now.'

It was never that simple, and I feel that their doubt and concern were my first indelible memory of spoken words. And being responsible for so many things I could not understand.

32. NATIVE SIGNER – NATIVE SPEAKER

A shared house soon became too small for our family of three. City living had been convenient during the war, with both my parents employed until I came along. Everything was on a tram or train line back to their family or community, but they did not want to be a Deaf couple relying on others. They also knew they wanted more children, and they were ready to build their own future.

Eve still had the three-hundred-pound inheritance left to her by her father. It was a small nest egg for a careful couple. Deaf beach picnics were regular events for my parents, so they were familiar with the beachside suburbs between Carrum and Chelsea. Their plan was to live close to the beach, and my father would build our house. With Eve's legacy and some savings, they bought a quarter-acre block of land in Fowler Street, Bonbeach, on the border of Chelsea. They always planned ahead: it was a ten-minute walk to the beach, a fifteen-minute walk to the shops and train station and a five-minute walk to the primary school. But being close to the beach was the best part of their dream location.

Before they could build their home and family, my

parents needed to move closer to the area. Carrum was close to both the beach and the river. There they found a small, cheap house available to rent, and for the first time, we would be on our own as a family of three.

Beachside Carrum was the suburban outskirts. Settled near Carrum Creek (now the Patterson River), it was a town of fishing boats, river and sea swimming, a train station for trips to the city, a service station, shops, a health centre for babies, and at least four churches. At that time, people there were struggling to make ends meet. Carrum was a scattered suburb where scruffy kids wandered along the river, under the railway and road bridges, and were always ready to swim in the shallows of Port Phillip Bay. Time did not matter; they would find their own way home when they were hungry or too sunburned to stay away any longer.

The open sky, the muddy river and Port Phillip Bay were within a short walk of our home in Stanley Street, Carrum. We were on the Flinders Street–Frankston train line, important for easy access to my father's work, our relatives, the city and the Deaf community. The train trip took over an hour; the scenery out the window became part of the journey.

My father would ride his red bike everywhere when he wasn't catching a train. The new block was a forty-minute bike ride away from our little house; the weather never stopped him.

Cars were still a luxury mode of transport then, but Art did not drive. Some of my parents' Deaf friends drove, but only the men. The Deaf were a mobile community, despite being in scattered locations without telephones. Letters and cards were sent and, in extreme emergencies, even telegrams. Nobody questioned communication; it was organised and effective for the time. My father attended the Deaf Club weekly and brought home news, invitations, information and gossip to Eve.

My mother's sisters drove their own cars when they came to visit, usually once a year or whenever possible. My grandmother lived on our train line, but visiting her, or anyone else, was a full-day excursion. Dressing up and going out was necessary for my mother to stay in touch with relatives and the Deaf world.

My mother and I were often left alone to discover love, life and language together in Carrum. Most days were barefooted freedom. Living as an only child for a little over two years, I was immersed in the gentle knowing of my mother's small, strong hands. I heard her every sound, and she would feel mine. And for a short time, I was content in this perfect environment.

Eve had found her Garden of Eden, although there were no apple trees, deep dark dirt, farm animals or wide Bobinawarrah sky. Sand was everywhere, but with vegetables growing in the back garden and the washing flapping on the line, we were all living in paradise. A small house meant one thing would not change, and that was sharing a bedroom. My mother knew about keeping her family in her sights, aware of how an unheard child could develop a certain wariness about the world, and she would not have that for me.

***

'What is the sound of one hand clapping?' is a paradox posed to novices learning Zen practice. However, in my early life, there was another paradox – being both a native signer and a native speaker. I was able to hear something my parents could only feel – the sound of both hands clapping. People, including my parents, had been checking on me since I was born, clapping their hands near my head, everyone making sure that I was following sounds and was not 'deaf and dumb'.

Deaf or hearing, I was the centre of my parents' world. I listened, followed and pushed across every sound barrier. I was in training for a bilingual language marathon and they were my coaches. They encouraged me to reach the top of my game and push the boundaries of my full potential, however long that might take.

Both parents wanted me to have every part of my own language and as much of theirs as was possible. Hearing is a dominant sense in the gathering of language, although I didn't know it then. Outside voices would call me away from Deaf experiences and I followed sounds, just as my father knew I would.

My father could not believe his good fortune, having such a good-natured wife and a lively, feisty daughter. Other people thought they were lucky that their spirited child could hear and live in the world beyond their own. However, there were moments when my father was not so sure; he and my mother had gained much from the Deaf world, especially a sense of belonging and purpose.

Born a political man, he was an ardent supporter of Deaf education and opportunity. Justice was my father's passion, although he was often frustrated when he was unable to fly beyond his own deafness. Even though my mother had internalised her family's attitude that her deafness was a challenge and burden, she did not see the world as unfair. What was unfair was that despite her strong mothering skills, some people still doubted my mother's ability to raise a family.

Growing up between these two worlds, I internalised early on that my ears did not belong to just me – they were also my parents' ears in the community. I took my job and myself seriously. In my early years, I could not imagine my parents being in the world without me running the show. The difference between myself and my parents was often pointed out and, without realising it, that became my point of difference in our community.

33. TALKING HANDS

One of my earliest lessons was that the hearing world questioned difference and where it belonged. In my world, it was hard to know what the difference was, and why it would matter. We looked like everyone else, until we started talking on our hands.

Inside our house was all about hands – swiped, tapped, slapped, waved, flicked, clenched, patted or stroked. A complete language for all my senses, and everything was from my point of view. I was an open book with unruly hair, stamping feet, a pointing finger and a puckered forehead of frowning questions. My parents could read my every mood and each page was an adventure to them.

Outside noises happened around me, and my parents had their own way of teaching me how to separate sounds. They would quiz me as often as they could.

'What you hear?' my father would ask.

On one occasion, his index finger waved, pointed to me, tapped his ear and, in a horse-riding image, crossed the two first fingers of each hand.

'You hear horse?'

'Me hear horse.' What I didn't know was that he had

already seen the baker's brown horse while he was outside working in the garden.

Horses had many visual images for me, other than being ridden. I saw them pulling the baker's cart and the ice truck, and I had a rocking horse my father had made from scraps of timber. The sign for all of them was the same, though, and adjectives were new words to learn. There were signs for 'fat', 'thin', 'good', 'bad', 'clever', 'stupid' and 'funny', and for individual colours.

'My horse, make funny noise,' I told my father.

'Where?' he asked. I pointed to the metal rod that made it move backwards and forwards. He went into the shed for a can of oil. 'Better now?'

'Good.'

There was nothing my father couldn't fix. He knew what the problem was without even hearing whatever I had heard.

Colour and sensation were also my world. My mother did not have the language of colour until she went to school. However, I was only a toddler when I learned how to sign 'yellow', with thumb and first finger twisted on the side of the chin. 'Butter' was the fingers spread across the left hand; together, they were 'yellow butter.' 'Blue' was the flat of the hand rubbed across the back of the other hand, and 'sky' was pointing heavenwards: 'blue sky'.

'Your baby bath blue,' my mother would sign, to reinforce my learning.

Unsure whether it comes from faded photographs, my first memory is from around eighteen months old and based on sight, smell, touch and the hazy buzz of summer stillness. I was standing inside the large, white, chipped enamel bowl for my evening wash. The battered, blue baby bath was for mornings, or for playing in on a hot day. Buttery yellow twilight would brush across the walls of the stone lean-to that was our laundry-come-bathroom. Yellow came in different colours for the sunshine, gardens, beach and the washing flapping on a makeshift clothesline. There was another yellow, smudged with smoky spirals from the lamplight as the oily smell of kerosene evaporated in the soft breeze. Early evening was a golden glow and soft touches on bare skin.

So many iconic smells, colours, textures and shapes belonged inside my world and, still today, particular perfumes transport me back to how my senses were stimulated in my childhood.

When my mother would tap her two fingers to her nose for 'smell', then hold up the smooth, amber bar of honey-scented Pears soap, I knew it was time for my bath. After being washed with the silky suds, she would open the tin of Rawleigh's Ointment and release the lingering lime camphor and menthol smell of tingling skin and healing scratches. Unable to read the gold writing on the lid, it was enough to know the sign 'smell good'. It was one more scent that signified love.

I followed my mother's strong, tanned hands when the crook of her index finger would shake for 'soon', two fingers snapped near the eye for 'sleep', leaning her cheek on her two flat hands together for 'bed', her index finger for 'first' and rubbing her flat hand against her chest for 'bath'.

'Soon sleep, bed, first bath.'

In 1945, Eve had everything she needed: the treadle sewing machine made something from nothing, sunshine dried the washing, pride was a clean house and her happy child who would not stop talking in either language. Once again, at least for a moment in time, Evie was queen of the castle.

Talking on my hands told my mother how I felt, what I wanted, what I could see or smell, but never how things sounded. Some things could never be made from nothing. My mother would never hear what I could hear, and I didn't even notice until much later.

My summer playground was beneath the garden hose, where silver streams and sprinkles of light would entertain me and water the small vegetable garden. Background weekend sounds were my father gardening or building toys from scraps of wood: my rocking horse, and child-size tables and chairs.

Suburban seaside days began with washing sounds bubbling and boiling away inside the household copper, combined with the bubbles and smell of the pale yellow bars of waxy Velvet soap. The colours on the soap box were dark blue, yellow and red with white writing; my mother would point and sign each colour for me. The letters were distinct and defined, but I was more fascinated by how the letters were embossed onto the bars of soap. And what intrigued me the most was when my mother would scrub away at the soapy letters and they would disappear.

'Where go?' my talking hands would ask of the disappearing shapes.

'Gone,' she said, as the bubbles and letters floated away.

My parents never stopped exposing me to as much language as possible. Their particular way of making words gave me the familiar signs: drink, apple, sleep, play, come, eat, stay, home, bed, gentle, happy, funny, together, shop, pram, beach, talk, get up, wash, train, car, friend, mother, father, banana, bread, biscuit, hot, cold, tired, old, baby, chair, table, bird, dog, cat, car, horse, pig, butter, jam, smell good, smell bad and good girl (my very favourite one).

These signs covered everything I needed to know at the time. Although I was a verbal native signer, my parents did not want my language falling behind because they were 'deaf and dumb'.

My language skills seemed to be foremost in people's minds, but being at the centre of my parents' world was all I knew.

'Where father?' I would ask my mother.

My mother would tap her first two fingers on each hand for 'father' and both hands in a chopping motion, patting her chest. Copying her hands, I could say, 'my father work'.

'Father home before you go bed.' She would tell me, so that I wouldn't keep asking.

But most days centred on just my mother. She would notice when sounds alerted me, wave her index finger and ask, 'What you hear?'

My father would also ask these questions when he was home, teaching me to observe everything around me.

My language always began with pointing to things or to myself. I would touch my ear, clench my fist on my chin, and cross both index fingers: 'Me hear man talk.' I was proud to keep my mother in touch with the sounds of our street.

She would tap her first two fingers together for 'same', point to me, index finger down the nose for 'can', clenched fist to her chin for 'man', tap her ear and mouth, signing for me, 'Same you, man can hear, man can talk.'

Sounds and talking were not the only aspects of communication. Underestimated was how hands, faces and bodies can deliver clearer messages than many spoken words. Without anyone realising – apart from my parents – the main reason I was lucky was not that I could hear, but how my experience of language belonged across two worlds.

Easy to recognise was the hollow squeezing sound from the back of my father's throat calling, 'Dawn'. I was always close by. He would cup his hands towards his chest for 'bring', point to his chest for 'me', his hand a cup shape and tilted for 'drink', and I was happy to be responsible for him.

Inside, I would tap my mother's leg and tell her, 'Daddy want drink.'

'Good girl.' She would choose a big glass and not fill it to the top. 'Two hands hold,' and I would stagger off, happy to be in charge.

Our small, strong physiques showed we were hard workers. I was square-jawed, curious, idealistic and observant, like my father. My mother was energetic, stubborn and determined, and I was like her too, but in me her stubbornness was replaced with a relentless tenacity. It would have been easier for me, and everyone, if I had been born with my mother's good grace or patience in order to manage everyone's expectations, especially my own.

***

Exposure to the hearing world was more important to some deaf parents than others. Although I was a visual, spatial, tactile and curious child, these skills were not quite enough. Visits from my maternal family were welcomed by my parents; they both knew that gifts and good intentions would be carried across our back doorstep, even if they were mingled with concern.

'I'm worried that Dawn will never learn to talk,' was Joey's oft-repeated refrain.

'Mother, Dawn can say more words on her hands than most children can say out loud.' Gwen was concerned, too, but didn't want to fuel Joey's fire.

'That's all very well, but—'

'Dawn will pick it up by herself, Mother. She seems to be doing that already, she can say as much as most children. She's as bright as a button.'

'Thank goodness for that.'

'Evelyn dotes on her. She's not missing out on any attention.'

'I must admit she's already a chatterbox, but she still has to learn how to talk *properly*.'

'She's not shy! Now they've moved to Carrum, there are other kids around for her to play with. I've never seen a happier or friendlier child.'

'We don't want her with those rough children. But I can't be here all the time; there's no room for me to stay over and teach the child.'

'Nobody expects that, Mother. Although she's a funny little thing, it's like she already feels responsible for her mother.'

***

I heard and absorbed every word, and what I believed about myself were the words that my maternal family spoke around me. Nobody could have imagined how it was for a child like me, one who learned early to use people and places to measure my place in the world.

Living by the beach was a dream come true for my country-born parents. My father was seven years old when he first saw the sea, and he never forgot it. My mother loved the seaside and would take me there during the day to play in the water. When my father was home early, he would also come along and help pull the pram through the sand.

When our family moved to Carrum, that was when my sense of storytelling began. The multiple voices of Stanley Street wandered past, and instinctively I listened for them. Crossing between worlds was as defining for me as it had been for my mother. Now she would not be the last to know – she had her very own interpreter, and I was ready to begin a lifetime of gathering and telling stories.

34. MARJORIE PARKER

Every child needs a guardian angel. Mine was on the way, and she would be nothing like a brother called Leighton. A woman driving her own car, a first in the seaside suburb, but not a first for me as both my maternal aunts drove cars. This new woman about to take over my life was Marjorie Parker, or 'Mrs Parker' to me.

Taller than my mother and my aunts, her high bust would arrive first, followed by her dark features, firm jaw, brown eyes, dark wavy hair. Some voices seemed to pull slow and steady from the deepest part of the throat, in both the Deaf and hearing worlds. Mrs Parker's deep voice –the deepest I had ever heard, apart from Great Auntie May's – was the sound of a woman in control of her life with enough left over for others.

The demeanours of the women in my life meant different things to me. Everything began with my placid mother, but other influences were my gentle Auntie Gwen, formidable Auntie Adeline and fusspot Grandma.

Marjorie Parker was another type of woman; she was not a relative and she was not 'deaf and dumb'. Whenever Mrs Parker passed us on the street, she would wave and my mother would wave back. She would stop sometimes and try to talk to my mother. Holding onto the skirt of this tall woman was her little boy, who was my age. He had his mother's colouring, but not her resolute confidence.

Deaf women were already a regular part of my life, and they were always lively, funny, blunt and kind. The strange sounds of my mother's Deaf friends were as individual as any spoken voice to me. Deaf mothers were happy when they could get together. All children were welcome and I could be as feisty as I wanted. I played with their children, who were either deaf or hearing, and we didn't notice the differences that were part of language. Mrs Parker was about to change all that.

***

Language barriers would need to be crossed if Marjorie Parker was to include my mother in local gossip, make her laugh and reach out in friendship. They had both lived in the city and moved to the seaside, and were first-time mothers, so they already had a lot in common. Marge felt there had to be a better way of communicating than gesturing and writing brief notes. Bigger notepaper was the way, and she knew just where she could find some without paying for it. Up the laneway and along Station Street to the neighbourhood gathering place – the local butcher.

There was not a parting of any biblical seas, but the sawdust on the wooden floor of the shop would separate into dusty confetti whenever Marjorie Parker and her good intentions swept past everyone into Musgrave's Butcher Shop.

She called out with her husky, posh voice that would

make a dead soldier stand to attention, 'Good morning, Johnny. Can I please have some pieces of butcher's paper? Big, clean sheets. I need them to talk to the deaf and dumb woman, the one who comes in here with her little girl.'

'Good-o, Mrs Parker. I know who you mean. She writes me a note with her order. I always stick in a bit extra.'

'That's good of you, Johnny.'

'That little kid's a real corker! The way she talks on her hands with her mother ...'

'She is, but she needs to learn how to speak properly, too. She will be coming over each morning so I can teach her, alongside Gary. She already picks up words and sentences quickly. I think it's because she has so much sign language.'

'Oh, I didn't even know that kid could talk ...'

'Well, she can.'

'What d'ya know. Wonders will never cease.'

'No, they will not, Johnny. Thanks for the paper.'

'Anytime. I'm happy to help.'

All kinds would go into the shop, but there was no-one quite like Marjorie Parker.

***

Midmorning, I heard strong and small footsteps coming around to the back door and signed to my mother, 'Lady with boy coming.'

'Good, you can play with boy.'

'Hello, Dawn. I've brought Gary to play with you.' So now I knew his name.

Her ample arms were full with a brown paper bag of biscuits, a bundle of butcher's paper and a handful of pencils. Mrs Parker, with Gary holding her skirt, had arrived ready to interrupt my mother's routine and include her in local gossip. The kettle went on and Mrs Parker shooed Gary and me outside.

'Playtime, children, off you go. But listen to me, both of you, don't you dare go outside this yard.'

It was a change to my routine, too, but I was quick to adapt. We had a biscuit each, a sandy yard, warm sun and homemade toys, and I had a shy, hearing playmate who was happy to be bossed about by someone other than his mother.

Almighty Marge swept into the kitchen and spread large, white sheets of butcher's paper across the table and the floor. The larger the paper, the more possibilities for their stories to be told. Armed with a pencil each, and a few spares, the two mothers were well prepared to share their individual experiences.

'My best friend from school and still now, her name Marge,' Eve wrote.

A good omen. A new friend with a familiar name, but this time she was from the hearing world and only lived five houses away.

'I will help Dawn with her talking,' Marge wrote.

'Good for Dawn. Art, me want her talking be strong.'

'She can come in the mornings and I will teach her along with Gary.'

'Thank you. Dawn like talking, we try, not same.'

'Dawn is talking well for her age.'

'You think? Make me happy, not want her left out.'

'I don't think that is going to happen.'

The universal sign of thumbs up did not need to be written down.

Everything about Marge was bold, even her handwriting. Although her heart was big, she could be a bit overwhelming for some people. Not for my mother, however, who was always a willing audience for any good story. And as it happened, Marge Parker was a natural storyteller.

Limited means were how everyone lived, but Marge's husband was a builder so their family finances were less of a concern. But for women like Audrey Smith, who lived in the back lane and had kids to feed but no husband, everything was rationed and money had to be found. For a woman alone who was funding family desperation, street corners happened in suburbia.

'Do you know the woman with the dark hair who lives behind your house?' Marge wrote.

'I know her, I wave to her.' While she had certain standards, my mother never looked down her nose at anyone, unless they were dirty. 'She always looks clean.'

Marge was frustrated and local gossip needed a safe place to fall. 'Len said I should give Audrey my new coat. It's very cold out there.'

'Len kind man to give away your coat.'

'It was my first new coat since before the war.'

'You like your coat?'

'I loved it.'

'What colour your coat?'

'Grey and black tweed wool, with black buttons.'

'Colour look good on you.'

'I thought so, too.'

'Where you buy coat?'

'Foy's in Melbourne.'

'Good store. Was coat lot of money?'

'I thought so. I had to save up for it.'

'What you do when Len told you give away your coat?'

'What could I do? I gave it to her.'

'You both kind people to give away coat. Will you get new coat soon?'

'I liked that coat.'

'That hard, when you like your coat. Bad shame Len could not give away his own coat.'

'Audrey wore my coat when she was standing on the corner waiting to pick up men!'

'Very funny! People might think you standing on the corner.'

'That was what I was worried about.'

'I think that funny, you think it funny now?'

'Well, when you look at it that way, yes, it is funny.'

'What Len say?'

'Len said it is important to be kind. Forget about what other people think.'

'Good idea what Len tell you. Not easy for woman like Audrey.'

'Yes, it is hard for women whose husbands didn't come back from the war.'

'Very hard. Children, no money. What else can she do?'

The butcher's paper expressed the many sides of friendship. Marge had her frustrations heard, Eve was included in local gossip and the story would not leave the kitchen. Not many people knew the full story and for once, Eve was the first to know.

My mother's soft breathy giggle could make anyone smile. When Gary and I returned inside, both our mothers were smiling. The floor had disappeared beneath sheets of scribbled butcher's paper. Written words became fire starters, ready to be swallowed by the flames of the copper. A growing friendship was still spread out, but the secret parts were screwed up into loose balls. Neither Gary nor I could read at that stage, but some things were best kept away from children.

'Don't touch those papers,' Marge said. 'They have to go in the copper.'

Opinions, gossip and friendship filled our kitchen.

Later, I was confused when I heard one of Mrs Parker's opinions. 'You could eat your dinner off Eve's floor.'

Adults said and did the strangest things. I could never understand why anyone would eat their dinner off the floor, or why they were both smiling about making such a mess.

35. LANGUAGE EXPECTATIONS

Curiosity, gossip and sign language presided over my world, but something more serious was coming my way. Letters had passed between my mother, grandmother and aunts. Eve's recent letters had been about her new friend Marge who was hearing, lived close by and had offered to teach me to speak.

The discussion about me speaking was endless between my aunts and grandmother. There would be someone else that could solve this problem. They were all relieved; a woman who met their high standards was better than they could have ever hoped for. Overlooked at times; my parents always had a plan or a solution for me to navigate the hearing world.

I could never understand why there seemed to be so much fuss about me learning to talk when everything I did revolved around talking. Either language suited me, and I would talk to anyone, whether they wanted me to or not.

Hand in hand with my mother, down the unsealed road, past four houses to the Parker house. Whenever I looked back, my house was always in view. To me, that was as important as learning to talk.

'Me see my house.'

'You stay morning.'

'Why?'

'You learn talk.'

'Me can talk.'

'You want hear, with talk.'

'What different with talk?

'One day you know.'

'Me want know now.'

'You learn wait.'

'When me go home?'

'Lunchtime.'

A full morning away from talking on my hands was too long.

'Come in, Dawn. Say goodbye to your mother.'

Gary Parker called Mrs Parker 'Mother', but in my opinion he should have been saying 'Mummy'. 'Mother' was what my Auntie Gwen called Grandma. My most important word, and I was already questioning the language of my own household. My maternal family always said 'your mummy' or 'your daddy' when talking to me about my parents. They were the words I used too, although the signs I used on my hands were also for 'mother' or 'father'.

The world of language that belonged to my parents could be too complex for the hearing world to understand, yet I understood their every word and touch.

But alongside Gary, those mornings were all about learning to talk. There were words I already knew how to speak or sign, but finding out how those words sounded or joined together slowed me down.

Mrs Parker asked me what I had said to my mother before she left.

'I asked, "When me home?"' I replied.

'Dawn, you need to say, "When am I going home?"'

That was the first time I found out you were not meant to leave out words when talking with hearing people, even small words. Most people I knew were just happy for me to be talking, especially me. 'Me' and 'I' were confusing words – they were both me, the same person. Maybe Mrs Parker wasn't as smart as everybody thought she was.

Mrs Parker was enthusiastic about life, and she believed that teaching me was another of her contributions to the community.

'Lunchtime, Dawn. It is time to go home now.'

Mrs Parker and Gary would stand at the gate and watch me run to my house.

The smell of freshly washed clothes meant that I was back with my mother.

'Me home, me miss you.'

'Big girl, learn talk.'

All that bother about a few missing words ... I and me always knew what my mother meant.

According to Mrs Parker, there were also things that children should not hear. 'Dawn, you must not listen to grown-up conversations.' This did not make sense to me. Even though the hearing world did not tell children everything, my most important job was listening for three. Talking on your hands was obvious and in the Deaf world, anyone could join in, even children.

Manners were another foreign language. 'Don't forget to

say "thank you", Dawn,' Mrs Parker would say. But 'please' and 'thank you' were the same in sign language, and my parents always knew which one I meant.

'Dawn, don't interrupt when I'm talking to your mother,' Mrs Parker would remind me again and again. Gary was a much quieter boy than me, but I decided that was his business, not mine. Interrupting my parents was how I got their attention.

The focus on my verbal language became constant. Although oral stories and children's songs were never imparted by my parents, on rare occasions Grandma Lloyd would sit me on her knee and sing nursery rhymes. Joey shared this experience with me, even as she knew I hadn't inherited her beautiful singing voice. She was disappointed, but it was outweighed by her relief that I wasn't a 'deaf and dumb' grandchild.

36. CHANGE ON THE WAY

Separation drove up in a cream-coloured Rover. The week before Christmas in 1946 my Auntie Gwen and cousins Delwyn and Ivan arrived at our Carrum house. Life was changing shape and so was my mother; she was very big and tired. At two years and four months old, I had never left my mother for any period longer than Mrs Parker's language lessons or playtime.

'Why fat?' I'd ask, pointing to her stomach.

'Baby.' That did not make any sense. A baby was what other people had; my mother had me.

There were still regular visits between my mother and Mrs Parker. There was a new baby sister for Gary, but his life had not changed much. He never left Carrum and his mother had enough time for him, in between teaching me to talk.

My life was about to change and I would not be in Carrum to see that happen. Auntie Gwen was gentle with me, but I did not see her often enough to feel familiar with her, and certainly not comfortable enough to leave my mother behind. My mother explained these changes in the best way she could, trying to help me understand, but I had never left either of my parents before.

'You go holiday.'

'Me not want go.'

'You big girl now.'

'Me stay with you.'

'Holiday on farm.'

'Me want beach.'

'When come home, you tell me about farm.'

My maternal family floated in and out of our beachside world. My mother was always pleased to see them, but this time she looked anxious. Small notepads, my mother writing a lot. But she was not smiling, not the way she did with Marge Parker and writing on butcher's paper.

My clothes were not where they belonged – either on the line or stacked neatly in the bedroom. Instead, they were packed into a small case that was sitting on the table.

'Dawn, you're coming with us. Say goodbye to Mummy,' said Auntie Gwen.

Separation from my place of belonging was the biggest event in my life thus far, but clinging and crying were not going to change things.

'Dawn, don't upset your mummy. We will bring you home soon.'

I sensed 'soon' meant different things to adults and children.

'Me not want go,' I signed to my mother.

'You go holiday, good girl, home soon.'

'When?'

'Soon.' My mother hugged me.

'What you do me not here?'

'You see, surprise soon.'

'Why you cry?'

'Me miss you. Be good girl.'

'Come, Dawn, your mummy needs a rest and we have to get going,' said Auntie Gwen, though she did not want me to be upset.

'Don't cry, Lambie, you'll like the farm. There will be lots of things for you to do.'

There was nothing I could say. I wanted surprises and adventures, but only if I was able to sleep at home with my parents. Car rides meant certain things: new places, the smell of leather seats and carsickness. Now this trip would include wanting my mother.

***

Oxley Shire farm life was another world. Country smells were wheat, animals, manure and milk – a stark contrast to the sandy, salty, soapy smells of my suburban beach life.

The large farmhouse where Auntie Gwen and Uncle Charlie lived had two bigger girls and a boy. The eldest girl's name was Evelyn, the same as my mother. The best thing was watching as two big sisters showed me how to boss a little brother.

Whenever I saw my country cousins, they would make me the centre of their world. Not one of them could talk on their hands. No-one else could, apart from me. I had never seen a real cow until this so-called holiday. The sign for 'cow' was two fists making horns, a proper farm word. My cousins would say the word 'milk' for me to sign. When I squeezed my two hands together as if milking a cow, they would laugh and ask me to do it again and again.

Auntie Adeline ran the Markwood Post Office. Her husband, my Uncle Les, sold cars. His offices were in small country pubs. Head office was in the Milawa Pub. Selling a car could take a long time, sometimes well past teatime. They had three children – Ron, Lorna and Lloyd – who were all older than me. Uncle Les, with his black wavy hair and loud rattling voice, was my first memory of colourful language. 'Say bad words,' I would sign to make my father laugh. I didn't have any signs for 'bugger' and 'bloody'. My father liked Uncle Les – they would go to the pub together whenever he visited us in Carrum. Uncle Les also liked my father, who did not judge him for how he acted and spoke. Neither of them was a farmer, so they also had that in common.

What I loved about the farm were the knobbly grapevines covering the trellis outside the back door. There were verandahs on three sides and, with the blinds down, it was dark and cool inside. A milky smell filled the kitchen, from the custard, junket and ice cream that my aunt was always making. The yard was filled with chickens running around under the fig, almond, walnut and citrus trees. At night, they slept in the huge hay-filled sheds, and the next day we collected warm eggs. Those same sheds housed red and green tractors – Uncle Charlie's pride, passion and purpose. And outside, the heat ate the air and the grass dried up.

'Dawn is never still,' Auntie Gwen said to Adeline, sounding pleased with me. She would correct my spoken words, but not my behaviour. 'It breaks my heart when I see her crying for her mother, though.'

'She'll grow out of it, Gwen. We both had to toughen up before we were ready,' Adeline replied.

'But she's so tiny. No-one wants her to go through what we experienced.'

'That's the way it goes. We learned early how to get on with things.'

'Evelyn and Art are making sure that Dawn has everything possible.'

'Yes, they are. But they need to be careful she doesn't get too spoiled.'

'Oh, Adeline, you can be so tough.'

'Someone needs to be.'

Playing inside, I often overheard my aunts talking about me, and saying 'poor Evelyn'. What I overheard left me wondering about my perfect family.

***

The farm meant roaming free outside until mealtimes, when we would put our two hands together – not to talk, but to sit in silence. We bowed our heads before we ate, and waited for Uncle Charlie to say, 'Thank you, Father.'

Mealtimes at home were never silent or still. Flying hands shaped 'thank you' and 'father', words I had always known. 'Amen' was a new word which I could not sign or understand. I could sign the word 'finish' and that seemed to be the same thing, but it usually came after I had finished eating, not before.

If I put my two hands together, my parents would understand which uncle I was describing when I returned home. Everyone knew praying and swearing was the difference between my uncles. Whenever my father visited the Oxley Shire, he always knew going to the pub with one brother-in-law would be more inclusive than going to church with the other.

Early evenings were spent sitting with my cousins in the bulky lounge chairs, body restless. No-one expected me to sit still, except when Uncle Charlie was doing something called 'praying'. It was the same as 'saying grace' but took longer.

At Auntie Gwen and Uncle Charlie's house everything seemed to be watching over us. High up on the wall were two large paintings with valleys and cows. Near the fireplace, waiting to have a say, was my grandmother's polished Renardi piano. But my uncle had his eyes shut tight and he kept saying a name I had never heard before: 'Cheeses'.

On Sundays, we would go by car to the Oxley Baptist Church and sing the song 'Cheeses Loves Me, This I Know'. Singing Cheeses songs was new for me, and I already had enough love, whatever Cheeses said or thought.

Inside my uncle's church there were other new words and phrases, such as 'suffer little children'. My one previous church experience had been at the Deaf church for my deaf uncle's wedding. It was a sign language ceremony and I was not expected to sit still or stay quiet, and I was definitely not expected to suffer.

Comparisons were all around me. My mother was like my aunts in some ways, hardworking and kind, but she laughed more and she did not rush me. My cousins were country kids and I preferred the beach. My father did not pray or swear and, in my opinion at least, he was the most perfect Deaf or hearing man I knew. All these comparisons told me one thing: Carrum was where I belonged, and there had already been enough change in my life.

37. BIG SISTER

The weather was getting hotter and drier, so Auntie Gwen would take us to the river to swim. I liked feeling the silky water smooth on my skin and seeing the tree roots spreading into the brown water. But I preferred Carrum and the sea, with sand and salt rippling beneath translucent water, tickling waves, and trudging home with tingling skin. In the backyard, under the hose, I loved the familiarity of my mother's gentle hands washing me.

I needed to go home. Although everyone tried to distract me, I missed everything about my life with my parents. Then came the day Auntie Gwen told me that I had a baby brother.

'Dawn, your mummy has a surprise waiting for you. His name is Arthur Lloyd Hately, although he'll be called Lloyd. You're a big girl now; you'll have to teach him things.'

'When do I go home? I want to see my mummy and daddy.'

'Not long now, Lambie.'

Seven weeks was a long time for me to be away from my parents. I was happy to return home, even though I was carsick most of the way. Auntie Gwen had filled the car with baby clothes, homemade food, new shoes, dresses and a brand-new red trike, but the presents were not as important as what was waiting. My parents needed me. And any baby brother would have to be seen to be believed, at least by me.

When the long trip from Milawa to Carrum finally ended, my parents raced to the car. Each of them picked me up and hugged and kissed me.

'Good girl home now,' said my slim-again mother.

I was back on sandy soil with my parents where I belonged. And then all I could do was cry.

'No cry, you home now,' my father signed.

'Me want come home before.'

'Home now, you have surprise. Come see what you have.' Forgotten were all the presents in the car.

Soft shade covered a canvas bassinet. The first things I could smell were smooth soap, cotton and home, all outside in the fresh, warm air. Everything felt close and familiar, until I realised there was a new smell: the soapy smell of a clean baby.

'What?' I pointed.

My new world was being lifted up – me by my father, the flimsy net by my mother – and in the bassinet there was a neat bump with downy blond fluff. My new best friend.

Pointing to me, my father rocked his hand around his chest for 'baby' and rubbed his two fists together for 'brother'.

'Your baby brother.'

Talking on my hands, I pointed to myself and to what I could now see and believe.

'My baby brother.'

'You tell me when he cry,' my mother said.

'He good baby, little cry,' my father added.

'You home now,' said my mother, who could not stop smiling.

And that was where I intended to stay.

Then out came the Brownie box camera for photographs, to keep a record of all the changes taking place. Lots of photos were taken of my parents, baby brother and me on that day. Now a big sister, I had much to point out to my placid and interested baby brother, an easy target for my bossy ways. And now that I was home, I would not have to make sense of what I had overheard my aunts saying, 'Let's hope this little baby is like Dawn, and not like Evelyn and Art.'

What they still didn't realise was that talking in either language was second nature to me. It would be me teaching my brother to talk and sign. Mrs Parker's job was done and, as a big sister, mine had just begun.

38. SEASIDE SUBURBAN STORIES

Big sisters have to gather information, I decided. Although I had now spent some time in the country, it was closer to home where the stories were taking place. We were not country people; it was too isolated for my parents and for me. You had to drive a car to find out what was happening, and in Carrum I could walk out the front of my house at any time to find a story.

Across the road were other stories so different from my own, and I was intensely curious to know them. There was a fenceless house set to the side of the large block running between Valetta and Stanley streets. The dusty backyard faced onto our street and there were always children amid the broken furniture and machinery. In any weather, the weary mother, Mrs Fox, stoked up her old copper tub where everyone could see her doing her daily laundry.

My mother did her washing in her outside washhouse, but always in private, and she never looked weary, only happy, even with a new baby. When Mrs Parker invited my mother over for a cup of tea, I saw that she had a whole room for a laundry – separate from the bathroom, plaster-lined and with linoleum on the floor. I was impressed from an early age by the contrasts found in people's lives, laundries, homes and children; rich or poor, it didn't matter. But in my mind, there was a difference between Deaf and hearing stories.

My parents tried to say words for me, but I much preferred the many words I could learn in sign language. Beyond daily practicalities, my parents also taught me how hand shapes could bring animals to life. There was riding a horse, calling a dog, patting a cat, and 'greedy' and 'pig' were the same word. My two favourites were the cupping of the hand and sweeping it out like the trunk of an elephant – obvious and clever – and a monkey scratching under its armpit. These always made me smile. Everything seemed physically connected when you knew the shape of a word beyond what was spoken.

It was my father who taught me the sign for 'banana'. Holding up one index finger, peeling it with the other hand. He also taught me to use the sign and say the word together. But for a small child, some words were harder to say than others. Over and over, people like my Uncle Les would ask me to say 'banana' and laugh when I said 'bumama'. Until Mrs Parker stepped in and said, 'Dawn, don't say that word like your father taught you. Say banana'.

But she wasn't there all the time, and it was my father I turned to when I wanted to pursue stories that followed our language.

Although sign was my most significant language, it wouldn't always be. Without realising, I had already begun looking for other ways to discover what I thought was the full story. And that for me was through other families. Like the Fox family, who had the name of an animal, but it was a sign I didn't know.

I was guided by my parents – my mother liked people who included her and made her laugh; my father liked people who he thought were interesting; and I liked everybody, until I lost interest in them when another story came along. But for now, the Fox family fascinated me.

There was no-one telling the Fox kids to improve their manners or how to say banana. They ran wild and it looked like fun to me.

'I'll box your bloody ears if you don't shut up,' I could hear butcher-shop Johnny say to his younger siblings, but I knew he didn't mean it. They were playful words and not to be taken seriously.

I did ask my father why Johnny didn't live upstairs in the butcher shop, as I thought that would be a good place to live.

'Other family live there, he live in house near you,' my father told me. I already knew that house.

***

When my father arrived home from work, I would drag him to the front fence to tell him what else I had discovered.

'What want?' he would ask.

'Old house,' I pointed out.

'Your house old,' my father reminded me.

'My house good,' I said, and that made him happy.

'You good girl.'

'House have many children.' I pointed across the road again.

'You one girl, with one baby brother,' my father signed back.

'Look.' I didn't want any of us to miss out on the action happening in this unfamiliar family.

'You stay, can look, not go away.'

'Me stay here,' pointing to the spot next to the pine tree of our front yard.

At the same time, I heard the words 'rough children' in my head, the distant warning sound of my grandmother's voice, easy to ignore when she lived so far away.

'All look same,' I signed to my father.

The Fox kids did all look similar. They were blonde, blue-eyed and had prominent front teeth – 'buck teeth', they were called then. My parents noticed details about people and I learned to do the same at an early age.

One of the younger Fox children was a small boy around my age. Pointing, I would tell my father, 'Cheeky boy live there.'

'How you know?'

'Me know.' And that was the end of that story.

***

Families and their stories kept growing for me; I couldn't get enough of them. But the Fox family became of less interest once I knew that we would be moving to another house, the one my father was building.

'Try be good girl,' my mother was saying more often when I was at home. I thought I was, but now had more expectations with a little brother.

'Shh, baby sleep.'

'Be good girl, your brother learn from you.' He slept a lot, so I wasn't so sure about what he could be learning from me as yet.

'Beautiful, happy boy', signed or spoken, was how he was described by everyone.

I thought so, too. He was perfect to me, but I was waiting for him to grow up enough so he could follow me.

My mother was busy with my brother and the washing, Mrs Parker was old news and good manners, and I was ready to learn about new people and a new place. My father still thought I was a 'good girl'. But even when I wasn't, I knew he liked me being strong-willed.

***

Across the Carrum Bridge, a new family was waiting for me. With a red bicycle as our transport, my father built a wooden seat across the bicycle bar for me and my brother, although he was still too small to go very far.

Saturday mornings were my father, the shed and the red bicycle. Soon I was big enough to go with him while he worked on our new house.

'You want come with me?' my father would tease me. I wanted to go everywhere as long as I was back home by night-time.

'Big girl, me go new house,' I told my father.

To my mother, I signed, 'Me go work house.'

My brother never cried much, so I was not needed. Besides, I wanted to know what this new house was all about.

'Home lunch, remember afternoon sleep,' my mother signed as we rode off together.

When my father and I arrived at our big block, I noticed the framework and piles of timber everywhere. But something else took my eye: the house across the road was like nothing I had ever seen before.

'Look, big house.'

'Yes, big house.'

'Who live there?'

'Mother, father with children.'

'How many?'

'Four, might five, me think.'

'Same me?'

'No, you small, big children live white house.'

'Me want see.'

'Wait, very soon, I take you.'

Same old story, waiting took too long. I needed to be informed about this fantastic house and world immediately. And it was up to me to find out.

'How long before my house finished?' I asked. We were a growing family, so building a house should have been just as quick.

'Soon.'

'When?' One new word that seemed to cover everything.

At least time with my father meant things would still go my way. He wanted me exposed to places, people and language, especially when I was bluffing my way into a world that did not always include him.

'You want see who live in big house?' My father pointed and signed, already knowing the answer. 'Me take you soon.'

Everything about that house was outside my experience. White weatherboards, a big front verandah with cane chairs, and there was a small house on top too. I had never been in a house that had two storeys, and now there was one just across the road. Although the shops in Carrum had rooms upstairs where people lived, that was not a proper house in my mind.

'Me want go now.'

He gave in, ready with pen and paper to write on, and together we stepped across the road, went in the gate and walked around to the back door.

'Come in,' said a man's raspy voice. It was Jack Spence, the father of the five children – all older than me – who lived there.

'Hello, Dawn,' said Stella Spence, Jack's wife. She was a small woman, like my own mother. She already knew my name, seeing it written on my father's notepad. 'Come inside and meet two of my girls, Zenda and Julie.'

Curious and fearless, I sensed that I had arrived inside one of the safest houses I would ever know.

'You play, me work house,' my father signed.

I followed when Zenda, with her red-ginger hair, said, 'Come on, Dawnie. Let's see what Julie has upstairs.'

Julie had dark hair; I thought she was prettier than any other girls her age. She took my hand, and now I had my first big friends who weren't my cousins.

We passed through the large bedroom with a high double bed and I followed them both up the straight, narrow wooden staircase to find another bedroom with two beds beneath an attic ceiling. A bedroom for sisters.

The back window had a chair where something miraculous was sitting: a baby doll with painted brown hair wearing a long, smocked, pale blue dress. Even the fine hairline cracks on her ceramic face couldn't take away my wonder at the glassy blue eyes that could open and shut.

'I'll help you hold her, she's nearly as big as you,' said Julie.

It was the biggest doll I had ever seen, a story to tell my mother. The signs for 'doll' and 'baby' were simple, but I had no sign for the doll's wonderful name, and couldn't spell yet.

'This is Bubbles.' The name 'Bubbles' was a wonderful shape in my mouth. I hoped that would be enough for my mother to follow. If it wasn't, I would point to the bubbles in my bath later that night and sign, 'Same doll name'.

Zenda picked me up and took me to the front window. She pointed across the road where my father was busy building our house.

'Look, Dawnie, there's your daddy. You're going to live over there and be our neighbour.'

'You can come and play. Would you like that?' Julie asked.

For once, I was speechless. The Spence story had begun. They would always look out for me, especially when our family moved into our half-finished house. With this first taste of what was to come, I was ready to leave Carrum for bigger people with bigger stories.

39. LIFE MOVES ON

Hard work and owning a house were wartime outcomes for the hearing and also for the Deaf. But sometimes hard work alone wasn't enough, and both Eve and Art were grateful for the money Eve had received as a final gift from her father in his will.

The Bobinawarrah farm was kept running through the commitment of the flesh-and-blood heroes who remained behind when my grandfather died: my grandmother Joey, my Auntie Gwen and my Auntie Adeline. But, the war and circumstances changed the way the farm was managed, and Joey had to sell up. She needed a city house to live in, and after that was paid for, the leftover money was divided up among the family. Once again, a little more for Evelyn.

Without help and regular gifts from my maternal family, there would have been even more financial pressure on my parents, although they were both careful with money. But the farm sale helped provide the deposit on the Fowler Street land. It also meant my mother's family thought they had more say in the way our lives functioned. I heard their opinions and Eve and Art read their body language, so between us we sensed how they felt about the way our family was growing.

***

While we were still living in the Carrum house, our family grew again to five. My new baby sister was called Valerie Elizabeth. Her second name was after our paternal grandmother, Jean Elizabeth Hately. But I decided it was after our Auntie Beth – Uncle Cliff's wife. They lived in West Heidelberg and my two cousins, a boy and a girl, had their own bedrooms. I spent two weeks with them when my mother had Valerie.

Their red-brick house had a small, smooth, shiny, concrete porch that was painted a ruby-red colour, and a green lawn. It was not near the beach, but not as far away as the farm. While I was there, I made the most of being the centre of attention. I knew the stay would not be a long one this time; my mother would need me at home to help her with things she could not hear.

I was just over four years old and I noticed every detail that was important to me, but the brown radio sitting on the shelf in the kitchen was the best thing I had ever seen or heard. Everybody had a radio – rich or poor – except us, since my parents didn't need one.

Their front porch was where I first heard the song 'Goodnight Irene, Goodnight'. The Weavers were dominated by strong male voices, but all I could hear was Ronnie Gilbert's tuneful tremble through the house.

Sometimes I live in the country
Sometimes I live in town
Sometimes I have a great notion
To jump in the river and drown.

I did not live in the country; I did not live in the town. I lived near the beach, and furthermore, I would not be taking a great notion to jump into the river and drown. I was scared stiff to look when crossing any river, whether it be by train, car, bicycle or foot. But it was the first song I remember hearing and knowing where I was at the time and how it made me feel. And how much I wanted a radio for our family.

***

When I returned home I would be a proper big sister, with a brother and a little sister to look after, whether I was ready or not.

My brother had stayed in Milawa with Auntie Gwen while our mother had Valerie, though he also spent some time with Adeline's family. He was a gentle boy, but hard to pacify when he was homesick. It was decided that Adeline would bring him back after four weeks away.

When Auntie Adeline brought him back, I heard her talking to Grandma. 'We wanted to keep him until they had moved into the new house, but he missed home too much.'

'Adeline, he's better off with Dawn to keep him busy.'

'I guess you're right. Those kids get so upset when they're away from home and I haven't got time for a carry-on. My own kids don't get any extra attention … but he is the dearest boy – you can't help but love him.'

'Evelyn does know how to raise contented children, I'll give her that. The new baby never cries either.'

'Dawn is too nosey for her own good, but at least she knows how to tell Evelyn what's going on,' said Adeline.

'The new house will be more comfortable for them, even though it's not finished. The neighbours across the road will probably keep a look out.'

Gathering information was part of my job. My mother's family all had different opinions about what should take place, especially how many children my family needed.

'Let's hope that's the last one,' I overheard Grandma say not long after my baby sister was born. Such a strange thing to say about such a beautiful child, I thought.

***

Our half-finished house in Bonbeach – with two bedrooms, a passageway, lounge, big kitchen and laundry – was big enough for our growing family, and it was time to move. Waiting for us was a larger house and a more populated suburb, still near the beach and even closer to the primary school. The move would be made with the help of Deaf friends, who always turned up.

I was learning – people, houses, families and stories kept changing – and I didn't know where anything started or finished. All that was left for me was to be like most people I knew and keep moving forward.

Our last five weeks in Carrum were the first five weeks of my baby sister's life. My brother returned after his four weeks on the farm. We shared the same room as the new baby and our parents. I slept with my mother to wake her whenever the baby cried.

Carrum had meant so much to my mother, especially the familiarity in her routines around the neighbourhood and in the community. It was a simple and free lifestyle, with room for her children to play, the beach close by, shops and the train a short walk away. A frugal lifestyle only made her more innovative in providing the best for her family.

But it was her hearing friend Marge who she would miss the most. For three years they had lived in such close proximity. Two young mothers with a lot in common: small children, new babies, milestones, gossip, humour, kindness and friendship. Language never came between them, and that was a rare thing in suburban life for my mother.

40. NED KELLY AND RADIOS

We moved into our new Bonbeach house just before Christmas 1948. There was more room for us to roam around in our own garden and in the street. Like Carrum, people looked out for each other. There was no Marge Parker for my mother, but with three children she was occupied and we did have Deaf visitors, and her family came now and then.

By this time, my father had started teaching me how to sign the alphabet: D-A-W-N.

'Big sister' or 'Dawn' is what my parents called me, but my brother and the Spences used my other name. 'Hi ya, Dawnie! Any stories today?'

I felt like I was already living inside one big story and no-one had even opened a book. Stories were not about being inside and sitting still; I had to go out and find them for myself. The important part was knowing where to look. I had overheard 'You mustn't tell fibs' and 'Now you're telling me stories', but in my opinion there was no difference between stories and fibs. Both were fact-finding pursuits to find a place in the hearing world.

There was one person in charge and it was me, pulling my bravado and my brother everywhere I went. Once inside other people's houses, my quest was to discover how all their stories informed each other, fitted together, and how I was going to retell them to my parents – or anyone else I could make listen.

Some stories were a long way from home, some were across the road or up and down the street, and one lived right next door to our new house.

'Me take brother see old man,' I signed to my mother. My father and I had met Old Tom together and now I wanted to introduce Lloydie to him.

'Not stay long.'

'Come on, Lloydie,' I called out. 'We're going to see Old Tom, but you make sure you hold my hand. And let me do the talking.'

Hidden behind a hedge of unruly pines, away from the road and down the long sandy track, was the two-room shack with a yellow-orange light. 'Tom' was a new name for me, but I decided it must be an old name because the man who lived next door seemed so quiet, ancient and lonely.

'What wrong man?' I had asked my father.

'War,' my father signed. That made no sense, but that was a question for another day.

'Why man live one?' I asked my father. 'One' was my sign for 'alone'.

'Stickybeak,' he tapped his nose.

Questions were about finding out; being a stickybeak was another part of telling stories. We were sometimes given storybooks; there was no-one to read them to us, but I loved the colourful illustrations. Luckily other forms of storytelling were all around. Stories were spontaneous moments that came together without anyone realising, and always open to my interpretation.

We both stopped in our tracks when we saw Old Tom standing in the doorway. He was wearing a dusty black felt hat, pants held up by leather braces and a wool jacket over a collarless, oatmeal-coloured flannel shirt. The smell of old, smoky material drifted from his shack. He had seen us coming.

'G'day, kids,' said the man of few words. He seemed pleased to see us.

'We've come for a visit.'

'Does your mother know you're here?'

My bold belief hesitated for a short moment. 'Of course she does.'

'Bet I know why you're here. Come inside and I'll see what I've got for you.'

'We're not allowed to stay long.'

'Well, I better hurry up then.'

'Don't be scared, Lloydie,' I whispered to my brother.

A simple, kind and quiet man, Old Tom did not scare me as he shuffled across to the sideboard where he kept his secret jar.

'Take your pick.'

We each selected two of the white, pink or yellow boiled lollies that made our fingers and lips sweet and sticky.

'Say "thank you",' I ordered. My brother was not going to say a word unless I told him to.

'Thanks, Old Tom.'

'Well, son, I see you're wearing your best hat.' I could see my brother relax a little. The battered brown felt hat had belonged to my father. My shy brother and the hat were one – he would start and end the day wearing the crumpled old thing. He had also found a big white feather that now decorated the brim.

'You like that hat, don't you, young fella?'

'My dad gave it to me.'

'Well, you look just like Ned Kelly.'

'Who's that?' I asked.

'A bushranger.'

'My brother is not a bushranger,' I said. And Old Tom laughed.

When we left the house, Old Tom said, 'See you, Ned Kelly.'

Our house was right on the Bonbeach and Chelsea border, which meant my brother's new name became legendary across the two suburbs. The name lasted longer than the hat; all his life, most people would call my brother 'Ned'.

***

Free play was how we lived our lives. Our imagination rose with the sun and went to sleep when we did, exhausted, but always ready for what came next. Our house wasn't as quiet as people thought. We banged walls or furniture to get our parents attention and were not restricted inside or outside the house.

The Spences were always ready for a visit, and I would ask them, 'Can I bring Lloydie over tomorrow?'

'Of course, bring Ned over anytime.'

'His name's Lloydie.' Hearing grown-ups did not always listen when you tried to set them straight.

'No wonder he never has to say much, with you to speak up for him all the time,' Jack Spence said.

There were too many things to understand and always something new to know. I would never give up trying to find my place, but I was pleased that my brother liked his new name and his old hat.

41. STORIES IN ALL SHAPES-SIZES-SOUNDS

Radio voices were the only thing missing from my world. Whenever I had a spare moment, I wanted what others had – a radio. Even Old Tom had one, although he only listened to the horse races. The secret voices of the hearing world. Members of my mother's family each had a radio, but until I came along, no-one had told my mother what happened when you turned the knobs.

The Spences had a brown and cream radio, it was as tall as me, and it would be on most of the day with the soft buzzing of news, songs and serials.

I would cup my hand over my ear and ask my mother, 'Me go hear radio?'

A radio was what could entice me away from home, and the Spences never seemed to mind how many times I visited them.

Knocking on the Spences' back door, someone would always yell, 'Come in, Dawnie.' Everything they did was clever, and I could never understand how they always knew it was me.

I was unaware that sound was a pied piper enticing us into the hearing world and away from our parents.

My parents had a lifetime of experience of people turning towards sound and forgetting about them. My father would sign, 'Only natural turn to sound'. But it made him cross.

Silence had its own art forms: mimed performances at the Deaf Club, charades, visitors, and watching people in the street. And soon films would become part of our lives.

But before then, shadowy magic manifested a long-eared rabbit, a skinny-nosed greyhound, a flying bird, an elephant, a horse or a duck – and it all happened inside our kitchen.

'Watch the animals move,' I would tell my siblings as my father made shadows with his hands. The duck's eye would open and the rabbit's ears wiggled. 'Daddy is the best storyteller.' My opinion still mattered to them at that stage.

Some details required big leaps of faith on my part. There were so many gaps that needed to be filled in and sometimes there was only me to make the final decision. Biblical stories were told when I went to the Milawa farm, and that was where I first heard about the animal kingdom. At home, the bedside lamp pointed at our kitchen wall was the backdrop for our own animal kingdom, and I decided that must be the Bible according to our father. Although somehow, I understood that my father did not believe in going to church, unless someone was getting married or buried.

Whenever Uncle Charlie read from his big Bible, he would look straight at me and say, 'You know, Jesus was a man who could walk on water.'

'That's nothing, my father can tell a story on the kitchen

wall using his own hands.' I wanted people to know my father could do things other people would find difficult.

'Dawn, that is not the same thing.'

'I think it is.'

'You don't mean to be cheeky, but you need to think about what Jesus can do for you and your family.'

And there was nothing I could say to that.

***

Life was simple at Fowler Street. There were no prophets, but once a month there was a man with a voice louder than any God who would cross our doorstep.

'Hello, hello, anyone home?' It was the shouting red-faced insurance man, the one who knew nothing about silence or manners.

'Man for money here,' I would sign to my mother.

'Can anyone hear me?'

I had heard him, of course, along with everyone else in the street. The one thing that bothered me the most was people who shouted into the faces of my parents. Deaf did not mean stupid.

He would open the door and step into our territory, calling, 'Hello, hello, hello … Insurance Day.'

'Man want money.'

My mother would get her purse and take out a coin to pay him. He would fill out her card, pat his red forehead and shout, 'Hot today … See ya next month.'

All he had to do was write on a piece of paper or tell me what he wanted to tell my mother.

'Me not like man.'

The good thing about sign language is that you can say what you want, when you want – even in front of other people.

'Not worry, me save money, when you grow up.'

'Man stupid.'

'Not know better.'

My mother had more experience of the world than most people.

***

Dreams took up little room. There were other things to do, but there was always one missing piece in the dream I wanted for myself.

'Me want radio,' I said to my father.

'One day.'

'When?'

'When big girl.'

'Me big sister.'

'Not big girl.'

'When me big girl, me have radio?'

'Wait see, need money.' My father's answer to anything that was out of my reach.

More confusion. I was a big girl when I had to do things, and all I wanted was a radio so I could be like everyone else. Although I was in a hurry to grow up, there was a long wait ahead. The best present I ever received was a radio, but I was eleven years old before that happened.

Meanwhile, nothing would stop me visiting other household stories. One day Julie Spence took me around the Golden Avenue corner to visit the McCoull sisters:

Barbara, Betty and Joanie. Inside their built-in verandah stood something grander than a piano or a radio: a black pianola.

It was hard to explain and even harder to believe. A piano or radio was feasible; many people had one or the other, and some even had both.

I wanted to tell my parents about the thing that looked like a piano. I was astounded that whenever one of the McCoull sisters sat down at the instrument, they wouldn't use their hands to play the keys. Instead, their legs pedalled hard, a fat sausage of paper cut-outs would go around, and 'You Are My Sunshine' would come from nowhere.

'Lucky girl, hear music,' my mother said, when I told her my latest story.

'Big girl say me can come again,' I informed my mother.

'You can go when you want.'

Both my parents wanted me to have every part of my world, even if that meant they were excluded.

***

'Daddy is taking me and Lloydie to the city to see a picture starring Charlie Chaplin,' I boasted to Jack Spence one day not long after the pianola encounter.

'You're a lucky girl,' he said. Something I already knew, except when my mother was too busy to talk now that she had a new baby.

'When are you going?' Zenda asked.

'Oh, I forgot to ask. I'll go home and find out.'

'That's the way, you need to know,' Jack Spence laughed.

'When we go town?' I signed to my mother.

'Tomorrow.'

'Where we go?'

'Melbourne,' which could be read as the same place as 'city' or 'town'. Sign language always had a few meanings.

'How?'

'Go train,' the sign of a fist going around at waist height like a big wheel.

Trains were something I knew about and there was one trip still fresh in my memory. The Deaf Club held an annual Christmas party, which meant new clothes, presents, party food and Father Christmas. The theatre of Father Christmas – with his red and white outfit, snowy beard, black boots and belt, coming through the double doors of the Deaf club – lived up to my expectations, but there was one thing that shocked me.

'Father Christmas not deaf dumb,' I signed to my father.

'Why not?'

'He can't. Many children can talk.'

'Not all children here can talk.'

'Me do.'

'You know, many children have mother, father, brother, sister who deaf dumb.'

'Me not deaf dumb.'

'You lucky not.' His smile meant he was not cross.

'Me go play.'

'Have good time.'

There was something best kept to myself: I believed in a hearing Father Christmas. Street radios played 'Santa Claus is Comin' to Town' and musical stories were for people who could hear. Inside the Deaf world, however, everything seemed to be a celebration of one sort or another, the flying hands of people who were always happy to see each other.

42. A WORLD BEYOND

It was winter when my father, my brother and I took an important train trip to Melbourne. Our mother would stay home and, after the washing was on the line, our good-natured baby sister would get all the attention. Although I thought they would both miss us, nothing could stop me from being excited.

'What we do in town?' I asked my mother again.

'Me tell you, go pictures.'

'Who with?'

'Father take you.'

'Brother coming?'

'Funny girl, brother going.'

'True?'

'You know true.'

'Brother must come.'

'Always take brother.'

My brother was part of everything I did then, and keeping him up to date was another job I claimed.

'Mummy said that Daddy is taking us to the pictures tomorrow, Lloydie.'

'What about the baby?'

'She'll have Mummy to play with. We'll only be away for the day.'

'That's a long time.'

'Not that long... and I'll be there.' I was hoping that would be enough. My brother did not like to be too far away from our mother either.

'What me wear tomorrow?' I asked my mother.

'Warm coat.'

'Me not like coat.'

Winter was wearing the double-breasted tweed coat that I disliked, since the mousey grey-brown bulk slowed me down. My grandmother had bought the coats for both Lloyd and me.

'You show brother, coat look good.'

Shy, scared and excited, my brother would never complain about his coat. Knowing what I did and did not want to wear made me more like my mother than we both realised.

'What father do when home tonight?'

'Clean shoes, wear tomorrow.'

Shoes were lined up on the speckled enamel copper cover. Oily shoe polish was the smell of my father in the laundry. The tin lid had a funny bird with a long pointy beak and the letters K-I-W-I, a word I could spell but not pronounce. When my father twisted the silver butterfly catch, I could see squished orange-brown pinprick marks. The polish was brushed over all the shoes, buffed off with a clean brush and given a final rub over with an old cotton nappy. Pride in presentation was a job my parents shared, and that always began with well-polished shoes.

'Me have hair bow tomorrow?'

'You can have. Now sleep,' my mother signed.

Melbourne was evolving in the aftermath of the war; immigration had begun, and foreign people, new customs and unfamiliar languages brought a new otherness that was beyond Deaf difference. Australia was adapting to alternative futures and so were we.

The next day started early, with our mother dressing us and putting the ribbon in my hair.

'See, look good with warm coat.'

'We go soon?'

'Soon. Remember look after brother today.'

'Me will.'

'You have good day, good time. Go now.'

'See you when me come home.'

'You can tell me your day.'

'Me will tell you what me see.'

'Father, brother ready. Go now, have good time.'

Broadway was the long street on the way to Bonbeach Station. Near the top of the street there was something to see: the old, unpainted house. Everything was small and grey, including the canvas verandahs and the sandy front yard. Missing was the green grass or weeds mowed into a lawn like we had at home.

The house being old did not matter, lots of people had old houses. My interest was in the children who lived there. It was anyone's guess how many.

'Hang on, Lloydie, we're going past that house with all the kids.'

'Where?'

'You know, at the top of Broadway.'

'How many kids?'

'I don't know, but I want to find out.'

'Tell me when you know.'

'Hang on to Daddy because there are so many kids that if we get lost, no-one will know.'

'We can't get lost, Mummy will be upset.'

'That's right, so hang on tight.'

I pointed at the house and asked my father, 'How many children live house?'

'Stickybeak,' my father signed. 'Wrong stare.'

'They not know what me say.'

'You not stare, family very poor.' I could hear their radio, so they couldn't be that poor.

People stared at us when we talked on our hands. Money was short in most households, but 'very poor' was something different. Here was a family that could not all fit inside their dusty, grey house at the same time, and that gave me a lot to think about.

My brother stared too, his eyes wide and blond curls freshly combed.

'Lloydie, we're not allowed to stare.'

'Geez, that place doesn't have any windows.'

'We'll have a good look next time we go past. I'm going to count the kids and learn their names.'

'That'll be hard.'

'Not for me.'

'Need walk quick, catch train,' my father signed.

We arrived at Bonbeach Station and our father stepped up to the ticket box. There was a glass cage with a face-sized hole cut out. The short man in a dark blue suit with a matching cap asked, 'Where to?'

Our father was smart in his suit and new hat. He looked like other men until he pushed a piece of paper and brown coins across the highly polished brass dip in the counter. It was his inability to share the language of others that exposed my father as different.

Still, the station master thanked my father and handed over a pink-and-white two-way ticket.

My father nodded his thanks in return.

'Me want same,' I told my father.

'You not five. Wait, soon big girl.'

'Where stand catch train?'

'Best middle.'

Individual sounds were something I was familiar with. I could easily tell the difference between the footsteps of my parents. I heard the sound of the train coming before I could see it in the distance.

'Me hear train,' I told my father, not realising that he could also feel the vibrations.

'Me know, soon come.'

'Careful not stand close,' I told my father.

'Me careful.'

'The train's nearly here,' I told my excited brother.

It was rare that I kept any opinions to myself, but one fear would silence me. The empty space between the platform and the wooden step was dangerous and big enough for a child to slip through. My imagination raced to falling past grey concrete walls, hitting the large, hard stones and iron train track, and then being left behind, cut up into small pieces.

Stories I told myself about being left alone on the station

or, worse still, underneath the train, continued with every train trip. My erratic thoughts would then settle down, knowing our father was in charge when he lifted my brother onto the step, helped me up and stepped inside himself.

The train was deep red on the outside. Inside, the roof had a polished wooden ceiling, arched like a small church. The leather seats were dark green, worn smooth from lots of people travelling to the city.

We sat on the far side of the train, my brother and father across from me, and we each had a window seat. I preferred not to be sitting near the door opening and shutting every time we arrived at a new station. There was more to discover when I watched from a distance.

'How many stations?' I asked, once we were all settled into place.

'Wait, you see.'

'More than twenty?' I could already count to twenty in both my languages.

'More than twenty. Me tell you when twenty.'

Details waited to be noticed: the polished brass handles shining against the honey-toned wood walls, the timber window trims and everything else my eye could see.

'What for?' I pointed to the solid straps of looped brown leather swinging in rhythm with the train.

'When train full, people hold.'

'Why?'

'Not want fall over.'

'You do that when go work?'

'Sometimes.'

My attention returned to the polished door handles that reflected my face back as a funny yellow shape.

The first stop after Bonbeach was Chelsea Station. It was where our mother took us shopping. 'Mother best shop,' I pointed out to my father.

'Good girl you know.'

Hattams Drapery had the counters downstairs where my mother bought material to make our clothes and her own. Upstairs was an open area for the main office. There was always something to see there; the money we paid with and the invoice would be stuffed into a wooden cash ball and sent up to the office by a wire. We would wait for the receipt and the change to glide back down. Other shops had this system, but this was the Chelsea shop that we frequented regularly and that familiar dinging sound of their wonderful payment process made everything grander in my mind.

'Make noise,' I would sign to my mother.

'You hear, noise good.'

The train left Chelsea. We still had more than twenty stations ahead. It was cold, so the windows were closed. While I had never heard of it happening, another thing I kept to myself was that I did not want to be the first kid to put my head out an open window, then have it drop shut and chop off my head. It was far easier to kneel on the seat and look through the window at passing backyards and railway stations, each one different in its own way.

Until we travelled over the Yarra River.

'Me frightened water,' I signed to my father.

'No worry, me with you.'

My father travelled by train most days and he always came back home. The fear of going over bridges took up a permanent position deep inside me, but the big Flinders Street Station never frightened me. Stations and train trips always meant stories.

43. DIFFERENCE HAS A VOICE

Flinders Street Station had people everywhere and all moving in our direction. My brother and I walked on either side of our father up the stone-grey station ramp. The walls were shiny white tiles with a burnished red-brown trim. A multitude of legs marched forward into a city of men in suits and ties, and women dressed in their finest clothes complemented by gloves, handbags and best shoes. Most adults wore a hat. Everyone was going somewhere, just like us, although not all of them were going to the pictures for the first time.

'Stay close me,' our father signed.

'Hold tight, Lloydie.'

'I will, Dawnie.' His soft voice was hard to hear in the moving traffic.

We never needed to be told that getting lost would be more complicated because our father was 'deaf and dumb'. Names called over the loudspeaker would be of no help, but my father could solve most problems by writing a note.

The arch of the station clocks blended into the background as we crossed over at the Swanston Street traffic lights. The crowd kept merging, and I could smell beer before I saw the building known as Young and Jackson, the one with the big sign. Across the road, looking down its nose was the towering steeple of St Paul's Cathedral. My father was holding our hands, so instead of signing to him, I said to my brother, 'That pub stinks of beer. Pooh!'

There were richer smells of coffee and milkshakes coming along Swanston Street. All around us was a new world of colourful, brightly lit shops and Greek cafes with big glass windows. We stopped long enough at one to see its red vinyl booths and Laminex tables. It looked like a place for grown-ups, but I still wanted to go inside.

'Me want drink,' I signed.

'We late.'

'Me want go inside, want see.'

'One day me take you.'

'Today?'

'Not today, we not want late for pictures.'

'Look at that, Lloydie, Daddy said he would take us there one day.'

Everything passed at knee height, until we deviated down Little Bourke Street past Russell and Exhibition streets to have a quick look at Chinatown before we reached the cinema. There were red, yellow and gold colours, high gates and coloured dragons of protection. On the walls and inside the windows were stick shapes crossing over each other.

'What that?' I wanted to know.

'Chinese writing.' My father placed each index finger at the corner of his eyes and stretched them into slits. The Deaf world was a visual one, and whether signs were culturally appropriate was not considered then. Whenever my father had free time, he would wander the streets of Chinatown; as a Deaf man, he was always interested in difference and culture.

The details to be found in difference also appealed to me. Located on the busy main streets were the vibrant shops and to me, they made a city inside a city, filled with colourful characters all coming and going. But I preferred the Greek world of bright lights, friendly chatter, ice creams and milkshakes.

Our destination came into sight, the Palace Theatre, grand of name and architecture. With the war not long over, the cinema was a magical diversion from too many heartaches and that's where most people found an escape. Outside on the footpath, we joined the overspill of people queuing for tickets.

The first of anything was exciting, but especially that visit to the pictures with our father. Dramatic doors opened and people and cold air floated inside. We followed the crowd. The day was not even half finished and no-one was listening, but I said it anyway: 'Just wait till I tell the Spences ...'

Once inside, the coloured mosaic tiles of the foyer floor had me pointing and sweeping my hand from left to right across my mouth: 'Beautiful'. Two conversations at once, I was also telling my brother, 'Lloydie, look at the beautiful floor'.

The ticket box was in the centre of the foyer – shinier, brassier and glassier than any train station. This time, our father did not need a note. He pointed to a roll of tickets and put up one finger. When he turned our way, I heard the blonde woman say, 'Okay, they're under five, free entry.'

'Not pay us?' I asked my father.

'Me know, you not five.'

We watched the backs of well-dressed people climbing the majestic staircase. Details mattered to me and I can still remember the plush carpet with aqua and brown swirls.

At the cinema, carpet and stairs were for other people; we joined our tribe shuffling across the wooden floors. The stalls were grand enough for anyone.

Inside was the biggest place I had ever seen. The blood-red velvet seats were impressive; one was pushed down for me while my brother sat on our father's knee.

'Lloydie, watch carefully because if it gets very dark, we've got no-one to ask.' We always needed to know what was happening. We both had an eye for detail, but sometimes we saw different things.

'Where picture come?' I signed to my father.

'Wait see.'

Waiting, I could smell wooden floors, dust and the musky odours of heavy coats. Winter had a damp scent in contrast to summer's freshness. My mother had taught me the language of good and bad smells. She could smell everything, even the rain coming.

Another mystery was waiting behind that wall of red velvet curtains. In pride of place was a black grand piano. The lights were still on, but I was ready for the next stage.

'Where picture come from?'

'Wait see.'

'Me want now.'

'Soon, not long now.'

'Me want now.'

'Brother not ask all time.'

Out of nowhere, the lights went out. The screen was spattered with silver and the full house of shadows went silent. But there was enough light left over for me to sign.

'Where picture come from?'

My father pointed. Beams of light were channelling down from a small boxed window on the back upstairs wall. Another mystery solved.

'Shush, picture soon.'

I was shocked by what came first. A roaring lion lurched through a hoop, a map of the world spun on the screen and from a faraway place came the deep, staccato voice of a posh man. The news included pictures – more information for my father, who read the newspaper and often used his dictionary at home.

Another roaring lion announced the cartoons that came next. Tom and Jerry jumped through bright red circles, grinning at the audience. The clumsy cat and cute mouse raced, chased and outsmarted each other, but they were friends at The End.

Interval came – a disappointment until my father signed, 'You stay with brother, me buy ice cream.'

I relayed this information to Lloydic, and then we waited. The door was the only place I could look, hoping to see my father come back inside soon. He took longer than we wanted, but returned with ice creams, reassuring us both that he would always find us wherever we were, even in such a big place.

'When big picture start?'

'Soon, you see funny man move.'

The lights went down again, shadows traced patterns across the ceiling and the audience fell silent. There was a black screen, white letters and music.

Then, all alone, he wandered down the road: The Tramp.

There was nothing about the way my father looked or dressed that made him different from other men, only the talking on his hands. However, Charlie Chaplin's costume shouted difference: his baggy pants, old stick-swinging cane, tiny bowler hat, too-tight coat, crooked tie and oversized shoes. He had black caterpillars for his eyebrows and moustache, a beak of a nose, and his dark eyes were wise and sad. His clothes, face and the opening scenes foreshadowed how the world excluded the odd or the different.

Although I thought of Old Tom as a tramp who lived in a house, this Tramp was something new to us: he was a poet, storyteller, romantic, dreamer and comedian showing us humility, courage and grace; an outsider seeking a sense of belonging. Charlie Chaplin's creation was like sign language; he used his whole face, body and costume to communicate. We applauded the man bouncing back from risk, rage and retaliation. Clumsy and graceful, funny and foolish, but always fighting his way towards final hugs of kindness and forgiveness. All that, with not one spoken word.

Visual images told my father the full story; dialogue and music were for the hearing world, so my brother and I had both. In time, I understood these films were chosen because the man epitomised injustice, irony and vulnerability – stories that were always important to my father.

Charlie Chaplin and his films spoke out for my father and other outsiders. My father was often an outsider in a group of hearing people, such as my mother's family. This was strange to me – why they didn't know how to talk on their hands. After all, they were grown up and I was still waiting to start school.

'You like picture?'

'Good picture. Man funny, sad.'

'End happy, man have friends.'

'Good.'

'Home train soon.'

'Me tell mother what we do.'

'Good. Mother happy know you two have good time.'

On the train ride home, we stopped at Chelsea Station where they had a taxi rank. We were all tired, so a taxi ride was one more event to top off the long day. As we journeyed home, I had tomorrow already planned; the Spences would need to be told every detail of our Melbourne experience.

44. A STORY GATHERER

Gathering stories was how I organised my day. And outside my front gate, stories happened right under my nose. Shifting dialogues were hard to sustain, but I always gave it my best shot. It was a matter of knowing where to look, who to ask and what to believe. Stories didn't have to make sense to everyone, only to me, as I discovered other worlds beyond my family.

Jack Spence worked at the local plaster factory. It was close by, just up Broadway and through the railway line, so he finished work earlier than most people. Something to see was how he came home covered in a coating of white plaster. Before too long, he would come outside washed and fresh, ready to take up his permanent position standing at the front gate, leaning on his arms and saying hello to the people going past.

'G'day, Dawnie. Have you got any stories for us today?' he would ask when he saw me waiting and watching at the gate.

One story was larger than life – Bossy Jones, who, a few times a day, rode his old blue bike past our house. His big bald head was a globe of shiny suntan, his one outfit of navy blue shorts and singlet was worn in any weather.

No-one to my knowledge had ever seen him walking, and he never wore jumpers or long trousers. Everyone knew where he lived – by himself in an old shack at the bottom of Broadway, surrounded by brown swampy land where local kids caught tadpoles in the winter – but that was all people seemed to know about him. I was hoping for more than that, and hanging around Jack Spence was one way to find out.

'How ya going, Bossy?' Jack would say to him.

'Good-o, Jack. How's yourself?' Bossy Jones was strong, healthy and friendly, with muscly legs and meaty knees.

Bossy Jones rode his bike around and around in circles as he chatted to Jack Spence. Same time every day, so I would wait at my front gate. When Bossy Jones rode away, it was my turn to run across the road and discover more information from Jack Spence.

'What does Bossy do?'

'Just that.'

'What? Ride a bike all day?

'Yes, Miss Nosy Parker.'

'I'm not related to the Parkers.'

As far as I knew, Jack Spence had never met Mrs Parker, who still lived near our old house. There were times when she would drive her car to visit us in our new house, but that was when he was at work.

'Just a joke,' said Jack Spence.

'But you can't ride a bike all day.' Some grown-up jokes felt like being told off.

'You never give up, do you, Dawnie?'

'He must have a job.'

'Bossy's a bachelor, he doesn't need much money.'

'Bachelor' was a new word that I wanted to try out. I had heard of bakers, butchers and builders, but never a bachelor. There were no signs to ask my father. He would attempt to answer all my questions, but I needed the right words or he would sign, 'What you mean?'

'See ya, Dawnie … teatime.' Jack Spence was restless now.

'See you later.'

'Yeah, I'll see you tomorrow for another chinwag.' Jack Spence used another new word and I guessed it meant talking. But I didn't know how to sign it for my parents.

***

Midmorning, neighbours would gather for fresh bread and my new word, a chinwag. The neighbourhood was friendly, but they did not have Marge Parker's ability to include my mother in local gossip. That was my job.

Sound or smell, I never knew if the *clip-clop* of the baker's horse or the crusty smell of freshly baked bread came first.

'Me smell bread,' my mother would sign.

'Me hear horse, me smell bread.'

'You can hear horse?'

'Bread man here.'

The baker's cart would stop outside our front gate. A flat hand, with the other hand in a sawing motion was 'bread', a fist to my chin was 'man' and pointing to the ground was 'here'. Smells were obvious to my mother, but she would let me tell her anyway.

Visual expertise was my father, a Deaf man reading the

world, always aware of the smallest details, and he would show me how to do the same. We had been to a few films by then and my father was always teaching me to look for hidden details.

'When see film, watch man. Suitcase empty.'

'How you know?

'See how man walk, case not heavy.'

'Me can see.'

'Look, see no tea in cup.'

Once I learned the skill from an early age and knew what to look for, empty suitcases and cups would be the first thing I noticed in any film. My father built on that skill as he taught me. The baker's wife had twins recently and I was fascinated – although I did not want twin siblings, one at a time was enough.

'Two babies,' I signed to my parents.

'When you see twins, look careful, one always has bigger smile,' my father told me.

Written words were another minor miracle to me, both handwriting and sign writing. I was always attempting to write the letters my father was teaching me to sign. The details of the twirling, gold lettering on the side of the shiny, maroon cart that announced 'Carrum Bakery' were magical. The painted, curling, coiling sign was a bigger miracle for me than babies, even if they were identical twins, and I now knew how to tell them apart.

Meanwhile, watching out for the curious characters coming my way – such as Bossy Jones, the baker, the neighbours, friends and family – was expanding my repertoire.

Despite all the stories walking, cycling, driving or trotting past my front gate that I would take back inside to my parents and siblings, it was never quite enough. I always wanted more.

45. NEW DISCOVERIES

'Dawnie, you're going to kindergarten soon,' Zenda said.

'My daddy signs it as "little school".'

'That's right, a little school before you go to the big school.'

'What'll happen there, Zen?'

'Lots of things! But the best thing is that you will find out lots more stories.'

Zenda always had a good answer for my questions, and so did Julie.

Little school would mean checking on details and stepping into a world that did not include my parents or the Spences. My small case was blue cardboard with tiny pink flowers. It had a brown handle and a silver catch. Inside was the apron my mother had made for me and an apple. When I'd seen the case in Buckley's Gift Shop, I'd signed to my mother, 'Me want.'

'You can have. Big girl now, go little school.'

For once, I did not have to stamp my feet.

On my first day, my mother walked me to kindergarten, went shopping and returned to collect me. But everyone was exhausted from the day and the long walk home; something had to change.

'Me love little school,' I told my father when he came home from work.

'Tomorrow catch bus, go little school,' he signed. Buses were something my father knew about. When he had a drink at the pub after work on a Friday night, he would catch the bus home.

'Me go alone?'

'You can. Big girl now.'

'Me can catch bus.'

'Mother take you bus stop.'

'You know what time bus?'

'Me have timetable.'

'Me not want miss bus,' I reminded my father.

'Me fix. You can catch bus, enough time.'

My mother was the one to take me to the bus stop on the corner of Broadway, near the red telephone box. The first time, she tapped her ear and mouth to show the bus driver she was 'deaf and dumb', but she only had to show him the note once. The same driver was on every time. My job was to navigate the steps, my case and the fare money.

'See soon,' I signed through the window.

'Have good time. Me meet bus when you come home.'

The first time, I sat in the front seat near the door, and there was a lot of stopping and starting as more kids came up the steps, some with their mothers. The next time, I went further down the bus where I could see who was coming and going.

The bus from Grenda's Bus Services delivered me and the other kids to the white weatherboard kindergarten located behind St Chad's Church in Thames Promenade,

Chelsea. The day before had taught me nursery rhymes, story time, finger painting and how playing in the sandpit meant a damp bottom.

There and back for the first time on the bus. After kindergarten finished for the day, the bus stopped back at the Golden Avenue bus stop. My mother and two siblings were waiting for me on the wooden seat.

'Me catch bus.'

'Good girl.'

My mother was pleased to have me back home and happy with my day.

'Dawnie, you're back,' said my brother, and my baby sister smiled from my mother's arms.

'Lloydie, there was a boy called Billy Patton, and he giggles all the time.' A small detail I thought my brother should know because he only had sisters and so did Billy.

Over lunch, my mother asked, 'What learn?'

'Spider song, me teach brother.'

'Good, he happy you home now.'

'Lloydie, come on, I'll teach you "Itsy Bitsy Spider". It's like talking on your hands.' Our two languages combined without either of us realising.

Kindergarten was now my favourite place, and I would tell the Spences stories they had never heard before, at least not from me.

***

New discoveries kept coming my way, but one was a bit beyond my grasp. Whenever we went shopping, we passed the St Joseph's Roman Catholic Church, school and presbytery that dominated the corner of Station Street and Argyle Avenue, just near the railway crossing.

'All the Micks go to St Joey's,' Johnny Spence said.

I had no idea what he was talking about.

Rich or poor, Catholic or Protestant – all seemed to be different people. Just like in the Deaf and hearing worlds. In the late 1940s, my father impressed upon me his attitude towards Roman Catholics. There was a way he would *pfft* his face to show he was cross, but not with me, just the 'RC' sign. Our relatives were all Protestants, even the religious ones like Uncle Charlie.

Whatever the differences, I wanted to see a Roman Catholic up close. My chance came when two girls moved into a small house near us that faced into Golden Avenue. They went to St Joey's and somehow, I got myself invited to their house.

'Me go play with girls who have red hair?'

'Not stay long.' My mother was busy with our visiting relatives, so she was happy for me to be entertained elsewhere for a short time.

The next hurdle was accessing the house from the sandy laneway in our street. The fence was made from flattened kerosine tins, the gate was an old wooden door with a handle I could just reach. I opened the gate, then hurried past the rusty tin shed and the lopsided lavatory, unsure about who might come out.

Most houses at that time were designed with the back door close to the kitchen; we rarely went to the front door since that was reserved for formal visitors. This small house backed onto the back fence and had only one door that

I could find. I knocked and their dark-haired mother said, 'Come in.' She was smoking; I didn't know any women who smoked so I was already impressed.

I stepped straight into the lounge room and a miracle took place – I was stuck for words. Stare was all I could do. Paintings were on every wall. They showed a man with long hair wearing a white dress with a bright red heart, inside of which was a shining halo of golden light. The heart was encircled by barbed wire, and cherubic angels were flying above.

One wall had a safer image, a woman wearing a white embroidered tablecloth over her hair, a blue cape and a red dress. She had a haloed heart encircled with white roses and was holding the stem of a white lily. The Virgin Mary was her name, but that meant nothing to me, nor did the symbolism of purity. Jesus, the Virgin Mary and angels; not one image seemed to have their feet on the ground. There were four pictures and one was in a big garden called 'Paradise'. Overwhelmed by these images, I wanted to tell my father about the paintings and the red outside heart, but for some reason I decided that he would not want to know this particular story.

No matter if you were Catholic or Protestant, how many children people had seemed important. The Kennedy family only had two children, we had three (so far), and the Spences had five. Opinions about having children and Roman Catholics kept coming my way, but I didn't quite understand them. Suburban life seemed to have a lot of instances of us and them – something else I struggled to understand.

***

I was happy to leave that house and return home to see my relatives, even if it meant hearing, 'Dawn, be a good girl for your mother' or 'Dawn, tell your mother'. But I was just in time to overhear, 'Goodness, Adeline, people will think Evelyn and Art are Roman Catholics.' Trying to find out about Catholics still seemed relevant but beyond my reach.

'Oh, Mother, don't be silly. They only have three children.'

'The way things are going, there'll be more. Mark my words. I don't know how she'll manage.'

'Mother, Evelyn's going well with the kids. It's not for you to worry about.' Auntie Adeline's voice was low, but my hearing was perfect.

'What if the next one is deaf and dumb?'

It was hard for me to understand what she meant, since other people were always saying, 'Aren't they lucky all the kids can hear.'

'Let's wait and see if it even happens. Anyway, you had six children and you weren't Catholic.'

'Yes, well, that's what happened in those days.'

My grandmother always had a quiet, worried look about her. My mother noticed that familiar look and this time, she also read the concern on my face. For some reason, my grandmother thought my siblings and I were spoiled and lacked manners, so whenever she and my aunts visited, they would try to rustle us into shape. They had good intentions, but a visit felt like our world was being scrutinised and always left wanting.

'What say?' my mother signed.

'Grandma say nothing.'

My mother had always had a gentle acceptance about her life, but I was kept busy trying to work things out.

'Good girl, you can go play,' she signed. My mother knew I needed a breather from crossing between worlds. Although she could never provide the same reprieve for Grandma.

***

Without knowing, I had internalised my father's mistrust of the Catholics. The world always seemed divided: men and women, city and country, Catholics and Protestants, the Deaf and the hearing. Like children everywhere, with no-one to fully explain things to them, I began making up anecdotes for myself about how all these worlds worked.

After that monumental visit to the Roman Catholic house, I made my own connections between the smells and names of Roman Catholics. I didn't think I would be meeting too many soon, not with my father's attitude. The girls were called Bernadette and Pauline, and their surname was Kennedy; they smelled of milk, had long, thick plaits of bright red hair and they had scary paintings on their walls. In my mind, those descriptions would cover nearly every 'RC', at least until I found out something different.

Zenda Spence had ginger-red hair, but she did not smell of milk and did not have a Catholic name nor paintings on the wall, therefore she was not a Roman Catholic.

Entering other people's houses was about discovery. 'You, stickybeak,' my father would sign, although he liked my stories, except the ones about Roman Catholics.

46. N-A-M-E-S BY D-A-W-N

Names were the finer details in my life. My two languages crossed over, but names helped me make sense of people and places, especially when I was talking to my parents and looking for ways to belong in each world.

There was a difference between Protestant and Catholic names. Monikers like Mary, Colleen and Kathleen continued my idea about Catholic names, but names like John seemed to belong everywhere. The name St Joseph confused me – all sorts of people were called Joe, and my grandmother was called Joey, a combination boy-girl name. My grandmother told me her father's name was Joseph, but he could not be a Roman Catholic because she went to the Church of England and sang in the choir.

'Grandma' was 'old mother' in sign language. My brother was 'Ned' to our street, but never to me, my parents, our relatives or the Deaf community (although later on my sisters called him Ned). I never asked my mother why the name on his birth certificate was Arthur Lloyd, the same name as 'old father', my unknown grandfather. Arthur was also the name of our father Art, and the Lloyd surname did the rounds (we had an older cousin called Lloyd). As an adult, I wonder if naming her son Arthur was her private connection to her father, more than to her husband. Another unasked question that's too late for an answer.

At that time, the Deaf being known by a number instead of a name was not a story that I knew. It would have been impossible to imagine my parents as Girl 735 and Boy 587, or my mother's Deaf friends known only as numbers. They all had such pretty, friendly names like Alice, Betty, Frances, Gloria, Joy, Olive, Vivian and Winnie. And, of course, there was one name that was more like a full sentence: Marge always makes me laugh.

Pride in deafness belonged to my father, who told me many stories, but numbers as names was one he kept to himself. Much affection went into the naming of my father's Deaf friends, who he often called by their surnames – Noble, Puddy, O'Gorman – or their initials, such as GG for George Gideon or HH for Hube Howe. Joe Phillips was J-O-E. There was one friend who had the same sign as Melbourne; he was called Melby or Melby Dyson or MD. M-R-S Beard was the only woman on the Deaf Committee; her name used the alphabet and a hand swept down the chin like a beard – a name that suited her and always amused me. Her first name was B-E-R-Y-L or BB. I liked names that used alliteration (despite not knowing what it was called).

'Uncle' was a word I said and signed, but names were adjusted between the Deaf and hearing worlds, and depended on the way language was used. Some of my many uncles were married to my father's or mother's sisters, so they were all hearing. When I was young, my two Deaf uncles were 'father brother Bill' and 'father brother Wally' to me. They looked like my father, talked like him and had the same way of throwing their arms up in pleasure when they saw anyone from our family. They were a special kind of uncle, and I was fond of these two animated men who were so like my father.

Uncle Bill had a Deaf wife named Yvonne. She was an oralist with a squeaky voice that made me uncomfortable, but for her two hearing children it was what they knew. My mother pronounced the 'Y' as 'why', and that aunt was named 'Why-von'. It would have been simple to teach my mother that the 'Y' sounded like the 'E' in Evelyn, but I was not that far ahead yet in understanding how letters came together in either world.

There were only two uncles – Cliff and Evan – who were named as 'mother brother'. Uncle Charlie was hands in a prayer position, and the best one was Uncle Les: 'man say bad words'. My parents laughed when I told them that my little sister called 'mother brother C-L-I-F-F' her Uncle Kiss, and no-one corrected her because the name suited him so well.

Maternal aunts were difficult to divide into either of my languages. Their names and attitudes were too much a part of me. Whenever they were around, I never knew where I started or finished, and I thought my name was Dawn-be-a-good-girl-for-your-mother. My gentle mother's name was Poor Evelyn. Neither name made any sense to me.

Names were the starting point for learning how to sign the alphabet. While I took that very seriously, more general signs were often quicker, easier and familiar. The names of the Spences were in daily use. Zenda was 'big sister with red hair' and 'little sister with black hair' was Julie. 'Father of two sisters' was Jack Spence, Johnny was 'brother of two sisters', and tiny, smiling Stella Spence was 'mother of two sisters'. There was Joanie, the 'married sister not live there', because she lived around the corner in Broadway, close to the 'house of many kids', and Colin, who was in the navy, was named 'other brother not home'.

'Johnny had to get married' became the grown-up name of my third favourite Spence, but I had no idea what it meant. Another Spence had come along, his new wife Anne. I was disappointed that she wasn't wearing a white dress in the wedding photos they showed me.

'Cheeses' had a short life in my vocabulary. I was disappointed to learn that his real name was Jesus, but I didn't have to go to church or Sunday school, so it was a name I didn't need. Johnny Spence had said, 'Jesus Christ!' when the penny banger he was lighting for us one fireworks night went off in his hand, so I thought it must be a bad name and a word only used by grown-up men.

Names had their own language in our household. My parents always knew who I was talking about when I informed them of what was happening around the neighbourhood.

'Old man live old house', 'boy with red hair and glasses', 'girl with shop dress'. Homemade dresses were my world, unless I visited Auntie Gwen.

'Picture man walk funny' – we all knew that was Charlie Chaplin.

'Fish and chips man' was a rare treat whenever we saw him.

'Beer bottle man' was Frank Lightowlers, owner of the bottle-o in Golden Avenue.

'Pretty lady in big shop' was blonde, stylish Mrs Hattam from Toorak, who would sometimes work at the haberdashery counter, and she always made a fuss over my mother.

'Bread man' was the baker who had the identical twins.

'Cheeky boy mother' was Chooka Howell's skinny mother, who always appeared to be hitting him, which seemed like a waste of time to me.

Dawnelle's was the frock shop in Chelsea. 'Lady live corner house' could cover anyone, but we all knew it was Mrs Paterson, or Patto, and she was the only one who would call me Dawnelle. 'Girl play piano' was Nola, her daughter.

'Boy funny eye.' There was only one boy like that in our street, so my parents knew who I meant, but my brother always called him by his name, which was Barry.

There was also the family in Broadway with at least sixteen kids; I was never sure as they ranged in age from toddlers to young adults who were married and still lived at home, so I decided that there must be at least twenty. I was determined to learn all their names. It took me time, but I managed. I would call them by their individual names whenever I saw them. I knew the nickname for the whole family as well. Even though it was unkind, I would use that one behind their backs. Fitting in mattered.

Bossy Boots, Smarty Pants, Big Ears, Chatterbox and Stickybeak – these were also my names. But I didn't have time to bother with names that were about making me better behaved. There was always a new name, a new person and a new expectation about how to behave, so I just kept flying by the seat of my pants.

'You're a lucky kid, Dawnie,' Jack Spence would often say. I decided that 'Dawnie' was only used by people who liked me.

The Spence house had a passing parade of new name stories; they had a lot of cousins living around the area who visited them all the time. Zoe Staff was the Spences' dark-haired teenage cousin and she had the best name I had ever heard. Most girls were called Joan, Barbara, Janice, Carol, Susan or Lynette. Whenever Zoe turned up, I would make sure I timed my visit with hers.

'You know, Zoe, you and Zenda have the last letter of the alphabet to start your names.'

'That's right. They tell me that you've been learning to say the alphabet on your hands.'

'My daddy is teaching me.'

'That's good. Can you say Z-O-E on your hands?'

'Z-O-E,' I signed.

'Look, Zen, see what Dawnie can do? Do it again.'

And, of course, I did.

'You're a lucky girl to be able to talk on your hands.' No-one had ever said that to me before. Until then, I'd thought the girl who lived in the milk bar on the Nepean Highway was lucky. Her name was Antoinette, but they called her Toi. Her last name was Brain, but that was the unlucky part because some people called her Toi Brain, which seemed a cruel name to give any child.

'Dawn' was not an exotic name in my opinion, and I would pester my mother about it.

'Why you not call me D-I-A-N-N-E?'

She would tell me again how they chose the name D-A-W-N because they could both make the one-syllable sound. Everything about my birth, especially my name, was carefully planned to fit with my place inside their Deaf world. That meant I was lucky, but it would take me a long time to understand how.

47. TELEPHONES TALK BACK

The red telephone box stood on the corner of Broadway and Fowler Street, the same corner where I caught the bus to kindergarten. We never took things for granted, but most of the time the hearing world was on my terms and my role was to speak up for my family.

Neighbours were helpful when making phone calls, but I didn't want to be too dependent on others for help or favours. The hearing world never asked my family for help; we were more of a curiosity in the neighbourhood.

'You think can use phone?' asked my father.

'Me can,' I signed back.

'Me help you.'

'Me can phone.'

'Good girl.'

'When?'

'Tonight, when me home work.'

'Who me phone?'

'Grandma.'

I was always learning on my feet and my hands, but using the telephone was even more exciting than catching the bus by myself. My anticipation had to wait until my father arrived home from work, smelling of timber shavings and hand-rolled cigarettes. His first stop was always the concrete laundry tubs, where he washed away the day with Velvet soap. It played a big role in our family and mostly lived in the washhouse. My mother still used Pears soap for the babies, and it remained my favourite soap smell.

'Me have cup tea first, before we go use phone.'

'Hurry, me want learn.'

Phone calls were needed to make arrangements, and everyone knew talking was my forte. That first phone call was about planning a weekend visit to my grandmother. Joey Lloyd still lived around the Armadale area, but it was a long train ride and took some planning.

My grandmother's city house was a mixture of things – it was close to the front fence, had red brick with a stippled concrete verandah, smelled of furniture polish, had stained-glass doors and a tiny back garden lined with concrete paths and pots of parsley and mint. The centrepiece was the inside toilet. It had a wooden seat and a long chain that I wanted to pull when I could reach. Whenever my grandmother visited us, she would screw her nose up at our outside toilet. My mother scrubbed it every day with Phenyle Disinfectant and my father would cut neat squares of newspaper. It was behind the shed where no-one could see you. That gave me time to sit and think, so I was a bit surprised at Grandma making such a fuss about our outside toilet. It's what most people had, even the Spences.

As the eldest, I would feel excited, anxious and responsible when I overheard what was wrong with us – too spoiled, too shy, too talkative. Grandma was not unkind, her doubt was her own, but too many words settled into the sense of needing to do better, and if we couldn't, somehow it was my fault. In my mind, learning to use the phone would show her that we were also 'too smart'.

The best part of Grandma's house was the matching crockery, homemade fruitcake and red raspberry cordial. I loved visiting her. She had her own ways of showing her love for us, despite her anxieties.

And there was another highlight of Grandma's house – the black telephone that stood on the small carved wooden table in her dark passageway. She could use it to talk to everyone, apart from our family. I also knew we would never have a telephone in our timber house, so the telephone box was necessary for us to stay in touch.

'When ring Grandma?' I pestered my father.

'We go now ring Grandma.'

When we arrived at the red telephone box, someone was still inside. My father looked at the big gold-and-black letters. 'You learn,' he signed, and he began teaching me how to spell T-E-L-E-P-H-O-N-E. The sign for an old-fashioned telephone was much quicker, but my father took every opportunity to show me something new about language, especially how to spell.

He told me there were nine letters. 'Nine' in sign is the little finger held down, difficult for small fingers, but I liked how my fingers flicked out for 'ten'. Repetition, patience and vigilance were required. Then my father pointed to each letter and showed me the sign. It wasn't hard to learn, the shapes of the letters were the same in both my languages.

Tired of waiting, I went up to the small-paned window and looked through.

'Come back.' My father said, as he leaned against the fence, smoking a cigarette.

'Me want see.'

'See soon, learn wait'.

Once inside, the walls were dark green with black paintbrush smudges, and the box had the leftover smells of other people's bodies. The Bakelite receiver smelled like my father's paint thinners.

'Smell here.' I held my nose, but I secretly liked the musky odour of the grown-up world.

'Not worry, forget smell.'

Two thick phone books on the shelf were unnecessary; we were prepared with the number on a bit of paper. Metal and black was the box with the long silver buttons, one was 'A' and the other was 'B', the first two letters of the alphabet. Beyond me was the phone on a hook with a long cord. My father lifted me up to sit on the bench so I could reach the phone. His job was to take care of the money.

His instructions were easy to follow; we had talked about this at the kitchen table. When he lifted the phone off the hook, the buzzing sounds gave me a fright. I signed with my index finger spinning around my ear, 'Bad noise.'

'No worry, soon stop.' I wondered how he always knew what would happen when he couldn't hear.

He dialled the number. The phone was ringing, and then I heard my grandmother's voice.

'Hello, Josephine Lloyd.'

'Old mother,' I signed, and my father pushed the A button to take the coins. He already knew that if there was no answer, he would press the B button and get his money back. The thud of coins dropped inside the money box.

'Hello Grandma, it's Dawn. I'm here with Daddy.'

The phone breathed an empty silence. I was afraid that I had made another mistake, but then I heard, 'Hello, Dawn. When are you coming to visit?'

'I'll ask Daddy.'

'When go see Grandma?' I signed.

My father placed his hands in the prayer position for 'Sunday' and his finger on his chin for 'lunch'.

'We'll be there next Sunday for lunch.'

'That's good, I'll see you all then.'

'Good girl,' my father signed.

The telephone was a big step forward, but I wanted my grandmother to also call me a good girl. I had taken over another task that would help our family and proved we could manage, and I thought that might be another way to stop Grandma worrying about us.

48. BIG SCHOOL, BIG STORY

The story of my life was about to get bigger. The word 'luck' was still around and I was a lucky girl in either language because my biggest dream was about to come true. I just had to be patient until 1950 arrived. I would be the first one in our family to cross two roads to walk to primary school, and I already knew the way from watching the big kids who walked or cycled past our house.

Chelsea State School stood on three corners. The big double doors opened onto Argyle Avenue, and the even larger back gates were close to home. The impressive red-brick building had a clay-tile roof and a wooden staircase.

'I'm going to big school soon, and it's got an upstairs,' I proudly told Jack Spence.

'Start at the bottom, Dawnie, and work your way up,' he said.

'I already know the alphabet on my hands,' I told him.

'Hold your horses a bit, you'll have to do what the teacher tells you.'

'My daddy is taking me to see the school.'

'That's good. You'll know what you're getting into then.'

The playground was like a huge ship, covered in grey asphalt and pebbled stones. From the outside and up close,

I could see the school's big windows, chimneys and double doors. Seagulls swooped the empty schoolyard and there was the smell of rotting rubbish bins and old bananas. Scarier than the school were the brown timber shelter sheds. Later on, I found out that there were only two temperatures, hot and cold, and the back one was for boys while the front one was for girls.

Before I started school, my father took me there to get the feel of the place. The gates were locked, so we climbed over the fence.

'We get in trouble?'

'No trouble. Me write note, man comes.'

We walked from the back to the front yard. There was a garden in the far corner. Over the fence was the school tuckshop, 'Maccas'. Carol McCormick had been at my kindergarten; she lived in the house behind the shop, which was owned and run by her mother. I thought Carol was lucky, she could have shop biscuits whenever she wanted.

I forgot about comparisons when a detail caught my eye. Hanging from a tripod of timber, higher than the tuckshop, was a big brass bell. 'Out of Bounds', said a sign I could not yet read.

'What for?' I pointed to the bell.

'School bell, you not late,' my father signed.

'You have same when you go school?'

'Funny girl. You know me deaf dumb.'

'How you know go your classroom?'

'Teacher tell children.'

'Same when you big?'

'When me big, look clock on wall.' Although I did know

his life in a Deaf school had been different from mine, I was relieved to know that my father's world always had a solution.

'How long before me school?'

'Soon. Monday.'

'Who take me?'

'Mother.'

'Why not you?'

'Me work.'

'Mother have brother, baby sister.' I was concerned that my mother was already too busy.

'Mother, brother, baby take you first day.'

'Me can go self.'

'First morning. After, you can go self.' I was satisfied for the time being. I liked being seen with my mother and siblings, and we often went past the school when we went shopping.

Whenever we were out shopping, people would stop to look at my baby sister, a cherubic child with her wide-eyed stare and springy blonde curls. She was always smiling, yet ever watchful from inside the mushroom-brown pram. The heavy-duty war purchase was still up to the task of pushing children into sound-filled futures, especially with my mother at the helm.

'School good, you learn,' signed my mother later that day.

'Me want walk big school myself.'

'Soon. First day me take you.'

My parents were preparing me for an education different from their own. It was impossible for me to imagine that my parents had had a life before me – my mother's silent farm world, the country life that my father had shared with his many siblings. He had been 'lucky' that his world had included two Deaf brothers. Their Deaf education comprised reading, writing, arithmetic, carpentry, sewing and sport alongside sign language skills, the very ones I had known since birth. My education would also include singing, storytelling and walking home every day for lunch.

***

My stories were about dreams, challenges and the everyday. The pictures, my kindergarten, the telephone box, Wangaratta and the Deaf Club had all been conquered, and street stories continued to turn up at the front gate. Primary school would be a short walk to stories that would grow with me over the next six years.

'When me go big school?'

'Wait, soon.'

'You frighten school?'

'Stupid question,' I replied, and my father laughed.

'Not funny.' Both my parents knew me better than I knew myself.

'Good. You like go big school.'

February 1950. There was a new pair of brown shoes with small silver buckles waiting in their box. I was excited, but I was also upset; my hair had been cut too short and combed, and I liked it untidy.

Something I disliked about Oxley Shire holidays was how my aunts would cut my hair without asking. At least my mother always asked me, although neither of us could tell the hairdresser to stop. Like aunts, hairdressers had minds of their own. I wanted my baby sister's soft golden ringlets, the ones my mother curled around her finger. A battle of wills developed whenever the comb was pulled through my thick and unkempt hair.

'Look like lion,' my father would sign, and that was okay with me. Strong like a lion suited my sense of self. When Julie Spence had taken me to see *The Wizard of Oz*, the Cowardly Lion had exposed another contradiction to me: that brave and fearful could happen at the same time.

Uncle Les had said last time they visited, 'Geez that bloody kid can talk – she never shuts up.'

'Les, don't swear. Don't forget all the kids can hear,' said Auntie Adeline.

'Too bad none of you can talk to my mummy unless I'm here to help,' I said, but only under my breath so they could not call me cheeky.

'The kid could do with a bloody brush through her hair,' Uncle Les said. Although it was said to smarten me up, I was pleased that someone had noticed what was important to me.

Despite my hair having been cut and combed against my will, I was ready for school.

'What dress you want wear first day?' my mother asked me. My mother had spent the last week making me new dresses.

'Me want wear yellow dress.'

'Wear what you like best.'

My siblings and I were my mother's representatives in the hearing world. Keeping us all clean and well-dressed was her mission.

My father came home from work early the night before school started. At teatime, excited for me, he signed, 'My big clever girl.'

'Me big girl, go school tomorrow.'

Planning ahead was what my father did, and I would also need to plan for the morning. Someone would have to interpret for my mother when we arrived for enrolments.

'Tomorrow school, me talk for you,' I signed to my mother.

'Me take paper and pencil.' She already had my birth certificate and vaccination papers ready.

'You not forget.'

'Me won't.'

Even then, I knew that I could always trust my parents to navigate the hearing world on their own terms.

49. DREAMS COME TRUE

Every morning required organisation from my mother, but that was the least of my worries on my first day of school. I kept pestering her, 'Hurry, not late.'

Three spotless children were gathered and on time. The baby was sitting pretty in the pram, my brother holding one side and me holding the other, but I planned to let go when we were closer to the school gate.

'Please hurry, me not want late.'

'Learn wait!'

Two words often heard, but ignored most of the time. My strengths and my weaknesses could never be separated when I was ready for the next stage.

'Mummy, Lloydie and the baby are taking me to school,' I had told Jack Spence the night before.

'Aren't you a lucky girl. Will you be scared?'

'Of course I won't.'

'That's the way, Dawnie. There'll be plenty going on for you to keep up with.'

'I'll tell you all about it when I get home.'

'Yeah, I just bet you will.'

Bold belief was a new apron, chalk, duster and playlunch all packed inside my new brown case. The future was ready to open up with new people, names and stories.

Being summertime, we were nuggety brown and blonde-tipped from playing in the backyard or at the beach. I noticed that the people in our suburb would stop and stare at the beautiful baby, the blond boy and the bossy girl who all tapped and signed to our gentle mother. And as far as I knew, on that day I was the only child starting school who had 'deaf and dumb' parents.

The schoolyard was packed with kids, toddlers, prams and mums. My first image was of teachers ordering kids into enrolment lines. The words 'teacher' and 'boss' were the same sign to me: index finger and thumb shaken near the eye.

'Me want teacher, not boss,' I signed to my mother.

'Not worry, good soon.'

Everyone was grouped in rough assembly near the drinking taps and around the double back doors that opened into the enrolment area. People smiled at my mother and she smiled back. The women gathered, talked between themselves and my mother watched, touched and talked to her children.

Not long now before I would be there on my own. It was not like kindergarten, even though I could see Billy Patton with his straight black hair parted and combed. He was crying and hanging on tight to his big sister.

I wouldn't cry, although I knew I would be away for a few hours. The only time I wanted to cry was when I said goodbye to my brother. But I covered it up. 'Don't worry, Lloydie, I'll be home soon and tell you everything that happens at school.'

My surname started with 'H'; I knew the H sign was nearer to the front of the alphabet. My wait would be quick, not like Susan Young's.

'Hately, Dawn.'

'Me,' I tapped and pointed at my mother.

'You hear, you go now?'

'Come, we go.'

We trailed inside to the wooden enrolment desk and the waiting teacher.

The paperwork was passed over – my mother knew it would make people stare if she sounded out my name, so she pointed to me and then my name on the form. I was proud of everything about my mother, but I wished that she did not have to point to herself, then tap her ear and mouth, to show 'me deaf dumb'.

The news had arrived before we did, so the female teacher did not seem surprised. She said to me, 'Dawn, please tell your mother to fill in this other form and place her signature at the bottom of the page.'

After I signed the instructions to my mother, the form was completed. I noticed that people did not always look at my mother when they wanted me to give her a message, but I could also see that the teacher was impressed by my well-groomed and smart mother, who could read, write and talk on her hands.

'You go home now, me good.' I was feeling sad, but determined not to let anyone know. Next stages were my forte.

'Sooky bubs,' I whispered to my brother as other children started crying.

'See ya, Dawnie,' he said.

'You go, me good,' I told my mother.

I already knew that I would like school, but just then

I did want to cry. Instead, I joined the line waiting to go into the 'Bubs' area, although my first classroom was officially known as 1C.

'Don't worry, I'll be coming home for lunch.'

'Have good time.' My mother knew I could manage. 'Me go home now.'

Everyone in the schoolyard turned to look, and I knew that was because she was the prettiest mother in the whole school.

***

My first teacher was Mrs Maher. She lived over by the beach, and the Chelsea pub was on her street corner. I knew that because Julie Spence had told me, but suddenly I was not allowed to talk at school, even if there was a lot to say.

'Stop talking and follow me,' said the teacher.

Concerned about where to sit, I found a spot in the front row. As a big sister, a skim-reader, a chaser of details and a teller of stories, I was prepared for school.

'Now children, be quiet!' Mrs Maher said, clapping her hands to get our attention. A miracle: thirty-eight children fell silent.

Loud, bossy instructions were a new thing. Hearing adults usually took notice of me because I was the mouthpiece between them and my parents. Now I was just one of the kids.

Always thinking ahead, I was concerned that the children at the end of the alphabet had to sit in the back row. The smaller ones, like me, would not be able to see if they were stuck there because of their surname.

'Pay attention, children,' said Mrs Maher. 'Attention' was a word I had never heard before, so how to pay for it was another problem.

'Don't keep turning around,' the teacher said. Now I would not be able to see where the other kids were sitting, even the ones I knew from kindergarten.

'Children, sit still,' she said, and that was the final straw.

Teacher or not, she could not stop me thinking about my new classroom with a large window made from small panes of glass that looked out to the big grey gum tree and onto Glenola Road, where the bus stopped on the corner.

'Smell new green paint' was how I would describe the pale green walls to my mother after school.

'Eighteen girls and twenty boys are in this class today,' said the teacher. She was busy taking names and getting children seated. The room was pulsating with activity, time for me to gather details and even daydream while I waited. My father would ask me many questions about the day, so I needed to be ready.

Tall walls and high ceilings, there was a picture rail and centred above the platform was a painting. When the sun came through the window, wispy waves, smooth colours, soft smudges and the lazy sea were transformed into a mist of yellow-pink. Everything in the painting was alive: a small girl at the beach, wearing her cotton bathers and sun hat, was playing with a bucket and spade. I knew her – she was like me.

My mother was careful in the way she collected and collated a treasure trove of photos of her children, and many known and unknown people. There were numerous photos of our Carrum house, but there was a photograph of a younger me at the beach, so much like the painting on the wall.

'Me see photos again?' I would ask.

'Very careful, clean hands, sit table, look.' A brief hope that I would stop pestering.

'You know photo, me beach, with hat, bucket, spade?' I asked my mother after school.

'Me know photo.'

'School wall have painting, same me in photo.'

'You always frown in photo.'

'Me not frown,' I told my mother. She should know by now that was how I did my thinking.

Whenever the teacher said, 'Quiet now, children,' I would look at the painting. Someone else was always in trouble, even before they knew they had done something wrong.

'Sit down, Keith Ball,' the teacher would shout, but you did not have to be a teacher to know that was impossible for him.

I knew something about Keith she did not know. In the playground, the other boys called him 'Towser', and that was one name story I would be passing on after school.

'School, boy have same name dog' was the way I would need to tell my father. But that was difficult; it would not make sense to him, because I did not know how to spell T-O-W-S-E-R. By then, however, I realised that stories had many audiences, and for this big one, I had my brother.

'Lloydie, there's this kid at school who has a nickname, like you, but he's called Towser.'

'Geez, that's a beauty.' Strong praise, but my brother always knew what made a good story.

***

The first day of school had been a lot to take in. I had noticed, but not fully registered, the cloudy blackboard that filled up most of the wall. Along the top, sitting on straight lines drawn using the long wooden ruler, were letters made with the big box of coloured chalk: Aa, Bb, Cc, Dd for D-A-W-N, all the way to Zz. The big and little letters meant nothing to me, but talking on my hands, I could sign every letter of the alphabet.

Next day. 'No talking,' said the teacher again, so the second day looked like being the same as the first.

Names were an ongoing story for me, but I was not allowed to talk so there was no-one to hear that I could already spell words and names. D-A-W-N was easy. The harder names to spell were my brother's name, L-L-O-Y-D, and my sister's name, V-A-L-E-R-I-E. We never called her V-A-L, which would have been much easier to spell, and so would N-E-D. Difficult were the two Ls in Lloyd and putting the letters in the right order to spell Valerie. Spelling phonetically would have been easier – V-A-L R-Y – since that was how we pronounced her name.

Before I went to school, I could spell both their names and other small words; the sign letters made sense to me. But now there was another difference in language I would have to learn, and that was how letters could be large or small.

At home, it did not matter. Whenever I was talking to

my parents, I called my siblings 'brother' and 'baby sister', and, of course, the whole family called me 'big sister'. The spelling of names was a skill, but not necessary. We each knew our place in the family structure.

My parents and the Deaf still called me 'Dawn' in their own throaty ways; that I could always recognise.

In the hearing world, my full name was still Dawn-tell-your-mother. Only Mrs Parker still brought butcher's paper when she visited and spoke directly to my mother rather than through me.

'Don't be a show-off. No-one likes a show-off,' people would say. Show-offs usually had something to show, but at that time showing off needed to be put into its place.

My mother taught my little cousin K-A-Y-E how to spell her name, something she was able to show off to her big sister.

At school, everyone was too busy finding their place so they weren't yet interested in my signing skills. Talking on my hands was what I had to show off to the hearing world. I had taught my cousins signs for 'apple', 'boy', 'girl', 'milk', 'fat' and any other words they wanted to know. If I wasn't sure, words could be made up for hearing children (but Deaf children always knew, and signed, 'You say wrong').

What must be right were the written letters waiting at the top of the blackboard. Every morning, the first thing we would do was to sing the alphabet.

'A - B - C - D - E - F - G ... H - I - J - K - L - M - N - O-P ... Q-R-S ... T-U-V ... W-X ... Y and Z ...'

Pure joy was singing my heart out, something that was both familiar and new, and I lost myself inside the beat of the magic of letters and childish voices. There was rhythm, shape and symbols, and letters in different colours waiting to become words that could be used for telling stories.

When my father came home from work, I would tell him, 'A-B-C best, me know best, you teach me.'

'You lucky girl, not deaf dumb.' It would make me feel sad when he said that to me, but I didn't know why I felt that way.

In my mind, my parents had arrived fully formed. I took for granted that our family had two languages. The hearing school could only teach me one of them, but both languages required the twenty-six letters of the A-L-P-H-A-B-E-T. Something was missing in school language: the physicality and passion that was an integral part of sign language. But the voice for this family would not go unheard or unseen – as a native signer and a native speaker, education would begin with me. At least, that was my opinion now that I was at school.

50. E-V-E THE STORYTELLER

Six years old was the magic number when language worlds shifted and realigned for my mother and for me. School life introduced each of us to an extended sense of self, and anything seemed possible.

I had been immersed inside an extraordinary language that included honesty, beauty, theatre and skill. It was a far different experience from my mother's early family life on the farm. Now that I was at school, everyone assumed I was fortunate because my learning would take place through the same language as what they thought was used in the 'real world' – the hearing one.

Difference was other. Many people were uninformed, just as my mother's family had been when she was a child. There was one school of thought that the Deaf could be taught to talk, with time and patience needed to convert them to the 'natural' order of things. My father would express his anger at how the Deaf were not asked for an opinion about their own education. There was the never-ending debate and division about oralism and sign. Lip reading was assumed to be a complete language on its own, but the physical involvement required was often overlooked. Language in Australia was considered to be English, and it was a spoken language.

Teaching the Deaf simple words could be useful, but oralism as a main way of life meant it was possible to undermine language fluency and social connections. Many in the hearing world often thought that without speech there was something missing in Deaf communication. And there was, if they were isolated from language. Everything about a country childhood for both my parents meant many language limitations, even for my father with deaf brothers, but at least he had someone. It wasn't until many deaf children were six years old that they could fully share in language, start talking fluently, gain confidence and find a place of belonging in both language and culture.

At six, naïve and unaware, anything was possible for me and I thought that teaching my mother to talk was an achievable task. School had given me another level of bravado. But I knew without ever being told that I should never assume I could, or should, teach my father to talk. Language, culture and pride was how my father saw his place in the Deaf world.

Intuitively, I was aware of my mother's isolation in our suburban world. She was funny, vibrant and a good listener with her Deaf friends. Her family also knew that part of her, but it took more time with pen and paper. Sign language was something I was proud to 'show off' to anyone who was interested. Having been born a bilingual child intensified my language skills and appreciation, but I wanted my mother to also have what I had every time I stepped outside the gate: community connection.

I assumed another insurmountable responsibility and decided I would be the one to teach my mother to talk.

I began to look at ways to teach her, never realising that her family and the school had tried many times before. Success was difficult to measure, often leaving behind uncertainty and a sense of failure. The Deaf made sounds that left others uncomfortable. Listening was difficult enough, even with shared communication. There were language expectations for work and social situations. Even I, a child of Deaf parents, wanted to include my mother in a compromised version of language. Without realising it, I had adopted the hearing world's impression that sign was not enough. Furthermore, although I would never tell my parents, I had also reached a stage where I was often embarrassed by the strange sounds of some of their Deaf friends.

***

Intimate times with my mother started to disappear. Sharing her with my good-natured siblings had changed things for me, and every morning I would put on my bossy big sister dress and squash myself into expectations of responsibility. The day started with me seeking my place inside the hearing world; the Deaf world was the one I assumed I already knew. Hearing values dominated, so I strived to fit in with everyone else. Difference at that time implied 'never quite good enough'. At that young age, I was unable to appreciate the unique worlds I was crossing between.

Impressive stories still lived outside the front gate or across the road. The Spences were always part of my day, and it was important to keep them informed about all they did not know about me, my family and the world of school.

My favourite question to be asked, especially by any of the Spences, was, 'Got any stories for us today, Dawnie?'

'You betcha she has,' Jack Spence would answer for me, and they would all laugh.

'What do you want to be when you grow up, Dawnie?' Johnny Spence always asked the best questions.

'I want to be a teacher.'

'You'll need to be clever to do that.'

'Do you reckon?'

'Yeah, I reckon, but you'll be alright.'

'I'm going to teach Mummy to talk like me.'

Johnny Spence pointed something out. 'But you can already talk like her, on your hands. And you're not even deaf and dumb.'

'Dumb' was the word that jumped out whenever anyone talked about my parents and their friends. The Deaf world was filled with sounds – banging tables, scraping chairs, grunts, squeaks, sighs and throaty half-formed words – all recognisable and individual to me. If 'dumb' meant not being clever, that was even more surprising. Most Deaf people I knew were clever, as well as sociable, funny and kind, and they all seemed so connected to each other.

One night after dinner, in a rare moment, it was just my mother and me. The kitchen had been cleaned up, siblings bathed and put to bed out of the way. Thursdays were the Deaf Club for my father, and he went straight there from work. I would try to stay awake until he arrived home, needing to know he was back where he belonged.

On that Thursday night, I decided to teach my mother to talk. My father did not believe in oralism for the Deaf and his opinion mattered, but he was not home and my mother would never tell him. I wasn't too worried about what he would think; I already knew he was proud when I signed, 'Me love school.'

Whenever I was at home, playing 'Schools' was one of my favourite games. My father had made a blackboard for me, and I would sit my brother on a chair and say, 'Now listen to me, I'm the teacher.'

In my opinion, there was no need to be bossy when you were a teacher – you already had a captive audience. Jack Spence would sometimes still call me 'Bossy Boots', but I knew that it was a long time since he had been to school, so he must have forgotten the difference between being bossy and being a teacher.

There was also Bossy Jones, the happy-go-lucky man on his bicycle. He never said much or bossed anyone around, as far as I could see.

If I could find a way to teach my mother to talk, I figured that my maternal family would stop telling me to be a good girl. Instead, they'd see how clever I was. And they'd stop calling my mother 'Poor Evelyn'. Thinking back on this now, I realise that my mother picked up on my motivation for teaching her – she always understood my frustrations and passions.

'I know Dawn,' my mother would sign to her friends.

Despite the demands of all her children, my gentle mother could see that many of my frustrations were balanced by good intentions and a big heart. She would try to satisfy me whenever she could, but that was as impossible as me teaching her to speak.

People were not unkind to my mother. Often, they were very kind, especially to me and my siblings. People would smile and wave to my mother, but rarely invited her into their homes for a cup of tea. She was highly respected, but I wanted her to be included in the hearing community. They were all missing out on her gentle charm and cheeky humour. So many lost opportunities – my mother was good company in any language. Deaf difference created a distance that was crossed by using her children to 'tell your mother'. But Marge Parker had shown that a friendship on equal terms could be established – all that was needed was time, inclination, gestures and some sort of pen and paper.

The Deaf Club's Ladies' Auxiliary was held on Thursdays, but distance and young children made it difficult for Eve to join her friends for weekly visits. There were many missed opportunities for her to share in the stories of Deaf women and their children, most of whom lived in hearing suburbs.

Bossy Boots or not, someone had to take control in the hearing world, change perceptions and teach everyone a lesson about what was possible.

'Me teach you talk tonight.'

As a strong-willed native signer and speaker, and a naïve decision maker, I was confident that it would be me who would succeed. In my opinion, no-one had tried hard enough and, even more importantly, no-one knew my mother like I did.

The classroom was our quiet kitchen, and together we were cocooned in golden light. My mother slid herself along the bench first and I followed. We were both seated on the same side of the table and any distractions were sound asleep.

'Me want be teacher when me grow up.'

'Need be clever.'

What made people clever was something I could never understand. To me, my father was clever. I knew my parents thought I was clever, in fact they thought that about all their children. It seemed to me that compliments were withheld from children in most families. Although the Spences seemed to enjoy me, I would never ask them or people in the hearing world if I was clever – too afraid that the answer might have been I was not as clever as my parents told me I was.

'Me clever, you think me clever?' I asked my mother.

'Me think you clever.'

I knew my mother's family loved her, and so did I, but I had no idea if they thought she was clever, and I had never thought about her that way either.

On that first night of my mission, I had my mother's full attention. There was one word that I needed to teach her first. 'Chemist' was a word that came from deep within her throat as 'CHEM-ist'. 'Doctor shop' was the sign I used when we were out shopping.

There were times when I would check to see if other people had heard my mother trying to say words; I preferred her to sign when we were on the street. People would stare at her in two different ways: one, because she was so pretty, or two, because she was 'deaf and dumb'. The difference between judgement and appreciation was something I learned very early on.

My mother was a willing student and I was a patient teacher. She attempted every word we tried, and we both kept repeating them; repetition was how my father had taught me the alphabet in sign language. But the 'CHEM-ist' lesson was difficult for me; it just didn't work. If only I had known then how to explain that thinking of the letter K would have made saying the word easier.

The sounds of the Deaf world were familiar to me, and my mother's soft, throaty attempts belonged in my world. But I was still learning that her language had its own place, separate from the hearing world. The biggest lesson I learned was that what mattered most was having time alone with my mother.

***

Stories were never far away for me, and I soon realised that some were right under my own nose. Not the ones that belonged to my father, but the many silenced stories of my mother's Bobinawarrah farm life. Rare and precious time with my mother gave me the opportunity to see the world from her point of view.

Another Thursday night, my father not yet home and siblings in bed, my mother and I sat together on the kitchen bench again.

'What you do when you little girl?' I asked.

'Live farm.'

Since my failure to teach my mother to talk, there were things I could find out if I asked enough questions and she had enough time to answer me. I had a sense that her stories of the farm would be different from the ones I had heard from my grandmother and aunts.

Some children had parents who read to them, but the

teacher read to us at school and that was enough for me. There was a stillness in our household and, for once, I did not mind the absence of a radio. My mother had a childhood story for me, and I already sensed that it would be true and unique.

'You tell me story,' I asked her. She had her own way of storytelling that was different to what I had been learning at school.

Once upon a time, there was a sheepdog and a little girl who lived on a farm in Bobinawarrah. She had a father, a mother, two sisters and three brothers who all spoke in a different language to her.

'Me sit on fence,' my mother said.

'Why?' Stories needed questions to help them grow, and that didn't happen in school.

'Watch dog.' Her smile was soft when she signed.

'What colour dog?'

'Black white dog.' A folded fist brushed across the cheek for the colour 'black'; the colour 'white' was the first finger and thumb twisted on the cheek.

'You like dog?'

'Dog good friend.'

'Whose dog?'

'My father's.'

'When your father die?'

'Me six. After me go school.'

'You sad?'

'Always sad, me not know why he go away.'

'Where fence you sit?'

'Where can see my father on farm.'

'You like farm?'

'Me love farm.'

'You miss farm when go school?'

'Always miss farm. Good food and family.'

'What dog do?'

The storyteller's little finger swept on the lower cheek, the sign for 'sheep'. Two hands waved away for chasing or rounding up.

'Dog round up sheep.'

'You like watching?'

'Me look, me know dog clever. Chase sheep behind fence.'

One answer to what 'clever' meant. A thumb swiped across the forehead was the sign.

Now there was a twist in the plot: a silent child, without any language, sitting on a fence, observing her family farm world. I was the first to know that my mother knew the dog was clever to be able to round up the sheep.

Finally, I was closer to understanding how many versions of clever were possible. Clever or dumb or overlooked was how the world seemed to function at that time. My role in the family meant I was noticed. I was clever enough to be able to talk on my hands and, on this night, I was inquisitive enough to seek further understanding of my mother's world and how it impacted upon mine.

My father was always telling me stories and offering opinions about the wider world, and my mother took care of us. Suddenly I realised that my father was not the only clever person I knew; my mother was also clever. Growing up inside her world of silence, she always had been. No-one in her family had known how much she had seen, although I think Leighton must have guessed when he would say to her, 'Clever Evie.'

One of my biggest life lessons happened that night: how the words we use leave strong imprints on how we see ourselves and others. 'Deaf and dumb' was the language used to describe my mother, words that defined her as different from her family and the community. But it was in that moment that I realised how fortunate I was to have such a clever mother, who had never been dumb. She had one difference only, and that was to have been born deaf.

EPILOGUE: STORIES WE TELL OURSELVES

My hands remember. They have a language of their own. They are the small, busy, hardworking hands of my mother, not the long, elegant and creative hands of my father. My three sisters have his hands, and my brother's hands were an honest combination of hard work and creativity. My mother and father are long gone, but whenever they visit me in a dream, we still talk on our hands.

The seeking, the living, the teaching and the telling of stories has been my life's purpose. Many of those stories and the people in them have been underestimated or overlooked. But any good story has a mind of its own, however deeply it has been buried. Mine have been waiting for the right time and place to find a voice.

Technology is the language of the twenty-first century. The television news and other programs now present stories for both the Deaf and hearing worlds. The visual and cultural voice of Auslan is sending out loud and proud invitations. The Deaf are having a language party and everyone is invited. The venue is the screen of your choice, where an Auslan Interpreter is hosting language and cultural celebrations. And at this party, everyone is the first to know.

My two worlds now stand side-by-side. Growing up within my two language groups, one had the louder voice but the other could also be loud in a visual, physical and emotional way. Spoken language is my daily world, but talking on my hands has hovered in the background – a strong voice that refuses to be silenced or ignored by me any longer. For a long time, it was something that was easy to avoid, living in Western Australia a long way from my parents, but it was an intrinsic part of my being that was reignited whenever I saw the Auslan Interpreters or I met up with Deaf people.

Over the years, signs evolved and, because I have not been part of that process, my confidence in my signing skills is often challenged. The Auslan Interpreters enable me to revisit the signs I still know, engage with new signs and, without realising, immerse myself in a language and culture as familiar to me as breathing.

There are so many particular nuances, differences, peculiarities, idiosyncrasies and quirks from the Deaf world of my childhood, that now tell me whether a signer or interpreter comes from the same world as I do. Noticing these things is something that feels like a sixth sense to me, and a reminder that being born into the Deaf world has given me a wider understanding of how language can be explored and expressed.

There was a regular Auslan Interpreter on the Victorian ABC by the name of Daniel Hately. He is the hearing grandson of 'my father brother', Wally. Through him, my history and experiences continue to this day. When I watched the Covid news at home in Perth and saw Daniel, all the voices of my Deaf family culture would call me home. Daniel's slim physical appearance, understated body language, flexible facial expressions and elegant signing skills are faithful and familiar reflections of my uncles Bill and Wally, and of my father. I can see that, like them, Daniel has a generous heart. Knowing one of their descendants is now a hearing spokesperson for Deaf education and history would have made each of the Deaf Hately brothers proud.

The story of a hearing child of Deaf parents does not only exist within the parent–child relationship. What defined our family were ideas and beliefs about deafness that came from both the hearing and Deaf worlds. Today, there is a term for people like me, my four hearing siblings and for Daniel: CODA, or a Child of Deaf Adults, but that is not how I tell my story. I was the firstborn child of 'deaf and dumb' parents – that was the language used by both worlds at the time I was born, and later as I was growing up. It took a very long time for the term 'dumb' to be eradicated from the vocabulary of both the Deaf and hearing worlds.

When I turned twenty-one, my Auntie Beth, Cliff's wife, told me that my parents had been beside themselves with happiness when I was born. Learning this helped me through a time when I was confused about my own sense of purpose and place in my bilingual world.

School, suburban streets and country visits had dominated my early life. Two more sisters came into the family, so we became Art, Eve, Dawn, Lloyd, Valerie, Karen and Wendy. Five children in nine-and-a-half years, each one fortunate to have the individuality, creativity, diligence, humour, insight, acceptance and kindness of our parents. And it just so happened that we could all hear.

My childhood propelled me into early adulthood without

enough experience to navigate the terrain. I left school long before reaching my full potential and experienced early parenthood. I returned to education in my mid-twenties, something that was made possible by Gough Whitlam and his government when they abolished university tuition fees in 1974.

The hearing world came to dominate my story further after I moved from Melbourne to Perth in 1979. My teaching career was on its way by then, and talking on my hands only happened whenever I visited my parents at their Bonbeach house. Some things never change, though. Sign language still exposed me and my thoughts, as it does today. As a child, I was an open book and easy to read.

After six years, I took a break from teaching high school English and Drama and moved to the TAFE system to work with New Opportunities for Women (NOW). Schools, churches and community halls were our gathering places. NOW saw individual outcomes from the same programs and processes, groups making sense of personal and communal stories through journal-writing, reading, film, drama, discussion and poetry.

Little did I realise that I was surrounded by stories as complex as my own; the contexts were often different and the outcomes had taken other pathways, but every story was unique, including mine. Each new teaching environment was one step closer towards understanding the journey I had taken with my parents, and how it had affected my life. Past stories informed expectations, and every class was people skim-reading the room and each other.

I was naïve, idealistic and enthusiastic. And I never appreciated that being part of the Deaf world meant I had inherited an atypical curiosity and a particular demeanour to my body, especially my hands. When I went to work in a Perth women's prison, my story was closer to others than I expected. Beyond locked doors, waiting for me, was a reader of body language who would leave me lost for words.

Bandyup Women's Prison, on the periphery of the fruitful Swan Valley wineries and a lush landscape of hardworking lives, became an alternative teaching environment for me. There were rules and regulations for family, friends and a trail of do-gooders, each with their own agenda and opinion. On this particular day, my briefcase and I, both bursting with lessons for every situation, stepped through locked gates into the unknown.

I was met with the cynicism of a female guard with broad shoulders, a thick waist and solid calf muscles. Down passageways and past locked doors went an unfinished me, following from behind. Before the fistful of keys opened a brown door, she turned and said in her loud and clear voice of authority, 'Watch that M, she could charm the drugs from a drug dealer.'

The sun shone through the high windows of the cream-painted room. I thought the atmosphere was friendly enough. Nine women were ready for a break in routine. They placed the seats into a semicircle like I asked, and I took the roll. One name I called out was corrected.

'Her name's Turtle,' one of the women said.

Turtle was a tiny, timid woman with long, dark hair who only wanted to please, and she was hoping to be released soon. I didn't know anything about their crimes, release dates or past history. But often these details would filter through in time.

'Is that what you want me to call you?' I asked, turning to her.

'Yes, Miss.'

'Okay, Turtle, but only if you call me Dawn.'

In complete contrast, it was difficult not to notice M. Tall, wiry, with cropped hair and a sharp face, she was covered in silver chains, bangles, rings, necklaces and earrings. No-one else was wearing jewellery that I could see.

Her watchful presence dwarfed the room. Her intentions were clear, but my attention was elsewhere. She had placed herself on the far right, at the end of the row, where she could lean her grace, style, intellect and street smarts into the group or pull away. The perfect position for skim-reading me.

Key words and ideas were used to direct the free-flowing discussion. Students were free to pass if they wanted, but only M did.

'Pass. I have nothing to say.'

'That's okay, maybe next round.'

'Maybe I will and maybe I won't.'

'Fair enough. It's up to you.' The others had plenty to say, so that kept things moving.

'Dawn?' M had my number.

'Yes, M?' The other women were watching me and her.

'Oh … It's nothing.'

'Fair enough.' I had the group to consider, the session was nearly over and the rest of the women wanted to be heard.

'Dawn?' Everyone went silent.

'Yes, M?' I looked her in the eye.

'Can you … ?'

'What?'

'Can you … use sign language?'

A question from left field and out of context with what had been taking place in the group discussion. There was no doubt about who was in control, even if I had always been good at bluffing my way.

'Yes, I can.'

'Thought so.'

'How did you know?'

'Other people use their hands, but not like you do.'

M had chosen her moment with perfect timing. We needed to pack up; the women had strict routines. M had read the particular nuances of my face, my body, my hands and me. Although I sensed that she could only have done that if she came from a similar Deaf experience, I didn't fully understand it at the time.

Today, after so much exposure to Auslan Interpreters, I can see how M could have understood that unique part of me, my Deaf history that I had always thought was not obvious to anyone else.

I never did have an opportunity to hear her story because she dropped out of the group before the following week. Some stories remain unfinished in my life, as they should. Writing this book allowed me the opportunity to revisit how being the child of Deaf parents has left its mark on me, whether good or bad, and that is not always a story we share with ourselves or others. I had assumed that I looked and behaved like everyone else in the hearing world, but my hands, face and body still told a different story.

Over thirty-five years have passed since that day when M responded to my point of difference. When I first met her, freedom for M was in a distant future, which by now would have come to pass. I watch for her story in bookshops, the one M had to tell, but I have not found it as yet. I am still curious about the aspects of Deaf experience that we both shared and never had an opportunity to speak about.

***

My father died in 1984, three years too early to witness Auslan officially declared a legitimate language by the Australian government. Not so long ago – when television was a series of moving images, lips and half-finished stories – subtitles or captions were only for foreign films. The hearing world of entertainment and information was not one of inclusion, but, like so many in the Deaf world, my father found his own ways to cross over. His secret weapon was a lifetime sense of belonging with his brothers and friends. He had always lived Deaf and proud inside his own family, language and culture.

As a Deaf woman in suburbia, my mother had less flexibility. Once my siblings and I were older, she did attend the Deaf Club's Ladies' Auxiliary meetings on Thursdays, and often caught up with her long-time schoolfriends. But Marge Parker was a once-in-a-lifetime friendship that did not happen in that way again. After her husband of forty-six years left her behind, my mother's talking hands were often still. For a social woman like Eve, something was always missing – her farm, her family, her friends and, in the end, her language.

My mother, Evelyn, passed away in 1989 on Easter Sunday, one week before her seventy-third birthday. She simply went to sleep in her best friend's garden. Eve and Marge, lifelong friends, were side-by-side, just as they had been in 1923 when they first met as two little girls at the Victorian Deaf and Dumb Institution.

At the time of her death, Eve's children were scattered across the globe. Valerie was in Lesotho, Africa; Karen in Queensland; Wendy in country Victoria; and I was teaching on the Cocos (Keeling) Islands. Lloyd lived close by to our mother and was left to organise her affairs. We gathered for her funeral – all except for Valerie, as red tape made it difficult for her to leave Lesotho – and remembered the touch of our mother's hands and the love and pride in her heart. Each of us dealt with her loss in our own ways. It took me a long time to understand how broken-hearted I really was.

Evelyn's many friends, extended family, grandchildren, nieces and nephews attended her funeral. The one remaining Lloyd sibling, Evan, came to farewell his sister. What he must have been feeling I never thought to ask.

There had been a great deal of loss in the Lloyd family, much of it too early. Arthur had died in 1923 at forty-seven, Leighton in 1925 (not quite thirteen), Adeline in 1965 (only fifty-two), Cliff in 1975 (sixty-six), Joey in 1970 (eighty-eight), Gwenllian in 1984 (seventy-four) and then Evelyn in 1989 (just before turning seventy-three). Joey and Evan were the only Lloyds to live into their eighties.

After all Joey had been through, she lived to an older age than any of her family. After Evan's death in 2002 (at eighty-one), Evelyn's family – the multiple voices inside this story – were together once again.

***

Whenever I crossed into the Deaf world, I observed people who had a shared sense of belonging in a way that I have rarely witnessed in the hearing world. But that sense of belonging required a gathering place for all Deaf people. Today, Deaf meeting places and schools have been revised, repurposed and rebranded. The stories change and evolve as they continue to be rewritten with more input from all parts of the community. The Deaf are now included in the hearing world, and no-one is the last to know or miss out on an opportunity to reach their potential.

Society is now more informed, diversity in education is available, music and the arts are accessible, inclusion is an expectation, travel is straightforward, technology means more access, the NDIS is a support system, and the Deaf can separate and pursue particular abilities, passions, talents and skills through education, sport, the arts, travel, politics or anything else that takes their interest.

Personal history mattered to Eve; there had always been gaps in her story. She was meticulous in keeping photos, letters, articles and records of her people who gathered by Oxley Shire rivers, who shared her Deaf history and the treasured moments in her children's lives. Joey Lloyd was the one who first gave Eve the many photos of their ancestral history; it was the one language they both fully shared. These photographs and records completed the gaps in Eve's story and my own. However, for me it was also Joey's anecdotes that gave the faces and places a broader picture of my mother and her family.

Eve was much loved and belonged within her hearing family, but it was through her own language and culture that she found her strongest voice – with people who talked on their hands, were separated from families, and gathered together to socialise, celebrate, communicate, support each other, play sport, challenge attitudes and bring up their families. Through my experience of the Deaf world, and in the writing of this book, I have had the opportunity to reflect upon the many strengths and influences of the language and culture of my parents, alongside the influences of my maternal family and the hearing community.

Inside the Deaf world, I knew I was valued for who I was. There were no expectations from Deaf family and friends. My own expectations as a hearing child of Deaf parents included a sense of responsibility that was impossible to fulfil as a young child, however many stories I pursued.

Eve and Art also understood that I, as a hearing child, was born to search for my place in the hearing world, and that I would do that in my own way.

In the telling of my own story alongside my mother's, I have embraced the opportunity to reclaim the influence and impact my two worlds of language and culture have had upon me. The Deaf world was Eve's and Art's, not mine, but the love of my parents was, and always will be, my first language of belonging.

ACKNOWLEDGEMENTS

The sharing of stories requires a combination of open minds and hearts, and seized opportunities. My good fortune has been the belief and support from so many in discovering my own voice during the writing of *Unheard Voices*. Each contribution has been considered, valued and appreciated.

Throughout our twenty-five-year friendship, Sheryl Butcher has listened, encouraged, believed, questioned and supported me in discovering the depth of my own story, and celebrated every milestone of the joys, challenges and skills required in developing my strongest voice.

My friend Karla Law was the first reader of many early drafts for the sense of story, and asked pertinent questions about Australia's social history and the world of the Deaf. Karla has trusted in me for the length of time taken to write this book, especially when I wondered if I could last the distance.

Angela Italiano, my first teaching friend and one of the best listeners I know. I offer my appreciation for your close reading and editing of the full manuscript and your truthful responses. We wondered if it would test our long friendship; it didn't.

Thank you to other important friendships that have kept me believing and moving forward. There is my extraordinary friend, Camilla Mora, honest, loyal, funny and true, who can now say, 'I told you so'. Kath Moore, for having faith in me and offering many insights into belief and church rituals. Non-judgemental, another good listener is Carrol Western, who offers acceptance, hope and humour. On Easter Sunday in 1989, when my mother died, I was living on the Cocos (Keeling) Islands. Kay Warren turned up for me on that day, and she has been turning up ever since, believing in me, my good intentions, our friendship and this story.

Never forgotten are the many other friends from Victoria, Western Australia and other places who have all underpinned my past and present place in the world. Some are now missing from my life, but not from my story. Included are the teachers, staff and students who have contributed so many extraordinary life lessons. Each invaluable encounter is worthy of being included in another book.

An important thank you to each of the I-N-S-P-I-R-A-T-I-O-N-A-L women who have danced to their own music and shared hope, honesty, beauty, joy, kindness, friendship and laughter during weekly exercise classes, lunches and coffee catch-ups.

North Fremantle, where I belong, between the river and the sea, and the streets of friendship, diversity and creativity. Long may they continue. I am grateful for each person and encounter that crosses my path in this unique neighbourhood.

There are people who have generously offered their professional and personal input, and to each one of them I appreciate and value their expertise and encouragement. When this story was still finding its own voice, I met Iris Lavell. From the beginning, I have been extremely fortunate to have Iris as a mentor and friend to keep me writing and believing.

A visit to the El Dorado Museum gave me a chance meeting with Sue Phillips, who has been so helpful with Wellington family history.

Lisa Bayley, a loyal friend to my niece Rachel Hately, was passionate about this story from the start. Although it did not all finish up in the book, Lisa's expertise and enthusiasm for gathering historical information about my family helped to carry the story forward and saved me many hours so I could keep writing.

Bernadette Foley was the first professional editor to look at my manuscript, and it was her interest in the uniqueness of the story that kept me exploring my own voice.

One person who took my story and my confidence to another level was a wonderful editor, Sylvia Balog. Her expertise and professionalism were balanced with patience, integrity and respect. Every gentle suggestion allowed for me to discover a stronger and clearer voice. I will always be grateful to Sylvia for her heartfelt commitment to me as a client and as a storyteller.

Georgia Richter, from Fremantle Press, who picked up my manuscript submission late on a Wednesday afternoon and sent me a text early that Saturday evening saying she 'loved it'. A highlight in my writing process.

Rachel Hanson, Fremantle Press editor, who has kindly and safely guided me through editing as a publishing process. Her attention to detail and high standards have encouraged me to always keep the reader in mind and aim for a professional outcome. This was a challenging experience but, on reflection, one of the most important parts of the writing journey.

There are many people connected to the Deaf world whose input has been invaluable. Thank you to those people from the past and present who have given me clarity about aspects of a community which I had forgotten or did not fully understand at the time. My Hately relatives, especially Daniel Hately for his encouragement and support. The uniqueness of the experience in crossing between worlds has been enhanced by making contact with Cassie Rolfe, Marge Dyson's daughter. Cassie has reinforced my understanding of these experiences and explained how Deaf children were known by numbers, something I didn't know. For any details needing further clarification, Cassie would ask her Deaf cousin Diana (Sandon) Laing, whose input is much appreciated. Fiona Perry (Auslan Interpreter/Coda) and Marg Tope (Principal of Victorian College for the Deaf) both read the completed manuscript and made generous comments. I appreciate how each one of you has encouraged me in my aim for an authentic voice to represent the crossing between the Deaf and hearing worlds.

Shared histories belong to all Lloyd family members. Their many kindnesses to their Auntie Evelyn and willing contributions to this book are valued and appreciated.

My eldest Lloyd cousin, Evelyn Rayner, gave me historical information and the words our grandfather said to Evelyn when he left her at the Deaf School. Lorna Cheong informed the platypus and orchard stories, and donated our grandfather's Boer War sword to the Wangaratta RSL and his letters to the Australian War Memorial in Canberra. K-A-Y-E Lloyd, my thoughtful cousin, who has encouraged every step of the writing process, believed in me and the voices of our people. This book would never have happened the way it did without two natural storytellers and researchers, my cousins Gayle and Malcolm Graham. They promptly discovered every Oxley Shire link who is still alive and with enough wherewithal to remember significant details. Their humour, belief and support in much more than my writing reflects every open-hearted kindness that I remember from my Wangaratta families. To all my Lloyd relatives, I do hope my version of family stories encourages you to remember and reflect upon your own. Evelyn's cousin Helene Cook, who passed away on 9 April 2020, is remembered with respect and affection for her contribution as the 'keeper' of our Wellington and Lloyd stories.

Eve and Art would be happy to see their family turning up for each other, often in actions not words, but still expressing the love and belonging of our shared and individual stories. My sisters Valerie, Karen and Wendy continue the tradition of the Wellington and Lloyd sisters, always turning up to do what must be done with grace, humour and love. Rachel Hately, my niece who has championed this story from the start, you will always have a special place in my world. To my grandchildren and extended family of nieces and nephews, I do hope that in reading the Deaf part of your history, you will all feel proud of those who led the way.

The strong voices of my two daughters have taught me acceptance, to be a better person and to always see the funny side. Felicia will revisit her people through these stories and, together, we will always remember them and my eldest daughter and her only sister. Renay passed away on 29 July 2022, before being able to read the finished book, but proud to know that it would be published.

My love and appreciation always to my partner, Brian Kowald, who keeps me honest. He has believed in me and my story enough to take over the shopping, gardening and most things that keep our household running smoothly.

My brother, Lloyd (or Ned) Hately, loved a good story and his family; the heart of this book belongs to him. He told me six weeks before he died in Vanuatu, on 13 July 2018, 'You know, Dawnie, Mum's family loved us'.

First published 2023 by
FREMANTLE PRESS

Fremantle Press Inc. trading as Fremantle Press
PO Box 158, North Fremantle, Western Australia, 6159
fremantlepress.com.au

Cover portrait supplied by author; other photography: M. Hencher/Shutterstock
Designed by Carolyn Brown, www.tendeersigh.com.au

A catalogue record for this book is available from the National Library of Australia

ISBN 9781760992347 (paperback)
ISBN 9781760992354 (ebook)

Fremantle Press is supported by the Western Australian State Government through the Department of Cultural Industries, Tourism and Sport.

Fremantle Press respectfully acknowledges the Whadjuk people of the Noongar nation as the Traditional Owners and Custodians of the land where we work in Walyalup.

www.ingramcontent.com/pod-product-compliance
Lightning Source LLC
LaVergne TN
LVHW041110080826
845145LV00007B/1757

* 9 7 8 1 7 6 0 9 9 2 3 4 7 *